The
Section 8 Bible

Volume 3

*How to invest in
low-income housing*

VOLUME III

Also by Michael McLean

The Section 8 Bible

Volume 1

Volume 2

Volume 3

Section 8 Secrets

Metal Money

The Bulletproof Lease

CONTENTS

Preface vii

Chapter 1: The Hiatus 1

Chapter 2: Another Ball Breaking Inspector....................................5

Chapter 3: Lawn be Gone 15

Chapter 4: The Old Landlord was Sharp.. 23

Chapter 5: The Boyfriend 29

Chapter 6: Roaches...35

Chapter 7: I Panicked . . . and Made 3 Mistakes! 41

Chapter 8: Woman are Right, Men are Impossible 49

Chapter 9: Copper is the New "Ghetto Gold" 57

Chapter 10: Behr Paint, Most Improved Player 63

Chapter 11: 10 Year Smoke Detector.. 67

Chapter 12: New Locks – Less Headaches 73

Chapter 13: Vulkem Sealant 116..81

Chapter 14: Preventing Break Ins 85

Chapter 15: Landlord Tips 89

Chapter 16: Door Stop Alarm 93

Chapter 17: Toilets that Suck . . . Literally! 97

Chapter 18: Tub Surrounds 101

Chapter 19: Free TVs 113

Chapter 20: Get All of the Security
Money Before Move In 117

Chapter 21: Elimination 121

Chapter 22: Satellite Television 127

Chapter 23: Heaters, a Thing of the Past in My Book 135

Chapter 24: Electric Baseboards... 143

Chapter 25: Avoid Craigslist 145

Chapter 26: GoSection8.com 157

Chapter 27: Finding Good Tenants..161

Chapter 28: Pride! 167

Chapter 29: Playing Dirty, this time with Lawyers 171

Chapter 30: Fair Plan Insurance... 185

Chapter 31: Talk to Me!... 189

A Note from Mike on February 2020 193

Contacts.. 197

Dedication 199

It's been ten long years, but we're back again to save you some more cash and give you a few laughs!

Mike McLean

Nick Cipriano with his grandson, Dyryck

PREFACE

Finally, after a ten-year hiatus and thousands of requests from our readers, it has arrived. The Section 8 Bible Volume III is here! We're 50 years old now and we're a lot wiser and just as, if not more nuts than we were when we set out on this journey some twelve years ago and wrote Volume I, back in 2005. Never in my wildest dreams did I think that our books would be the precursor "how to succeed" book on Section 8 land lording. Never in my wildest dreams did I think we would be in our fourth re-print. Never did I imagine that some twelve years later, our books would still be enjoyed by folks breaking into or already involved in the Section 8 housing field. And for that, we thank each and every one of you who has ever purchased a book from us. Honestly, we couldn't and wouldn't have done it without you.

It has always been my goal to write books that educate, save time and money, and entertain my readers. I feel confident that I will be able to pull it off again here in Volume III, the Trilogy! I want you to enjoy the book from the time you pick it up until the time you put it down. I will give you your monies worth all the time, every time, that I guarantee. Most people write a book to make money, and all of you by now, know how much I like money, but honestly, I absolutely love writing and sharing my adventures with fellow or soon to be landlords. If I can motivate you, save you a dollar or an hour of time, or make you laugh at any time during the reading of this book, then I have done my job and that is exactly what I am striving for.

Alright, enough blowing my own horn and let's get to some real talk. If you have purchased Volume III, then 10 to 1 odds you have read both Volumes I and II. I'm also assuming that you've got a couple Section 8 properties in your portfolio or you are seriously getting ready to pull the trigger on your first deal. Do it! Cancel your flight from going nowhere and get in on this govern-ment money! Your dreams can only come true if you have the courage to pursue them.

I can't tell you how many people that I have motivated into getting started in this business. Most had 9 to 5 jobs just like me when they started out and are now up to twenty or more properties and have quit their 9 to 5. Some have added just a couple of properties and kept their full-time job. Look, I'm not going to break out the infomercial scene on you where the guy is sitting outback of his mansion at the pool, opening up $40,000 checks, it ain't that easy! But it's not that hard either. A little hard work and you're there. Sure, you can work hard for someone else eight hours a day, you might even eventually get to be boss —and then have to work twelve hours a day!

Most of the people's biggest fears who want to get involved in Section 8 rentals stem from the two words, "Section 8 ." They think, "what if the tenants destroy my property?" or "what if the tenants don't pay their portion of the rent?" Let me tell you this. Sometimes the cave you fear to enter holds the treasure that you seek most. If you're looking to increase your income enough to escape your job, I'm giving you the blueprint on how to get rich in Section 8 housing. I'm putting the keys right into your lap and all you have to do is take the risk or lose the chance, it's that simple and the risk is rather low. If it doesn't work out for you, evict the tenant and sell the property. In three words I can sum up everything that I've learned about life, it goes on, and so will yours. When I got started in this business, I didn't have the luxury of these three books and I still made it. I had determination but I didn't have experience. If you have the determination, I will serve you the experience on a silver platter. All you have to do is read and follow along.

Did you ever read a book and when you're ten pages into it you say, "Jesus Christ, the more this guy explains it, the more I don't understand it?" Well this is not that book! Nick and I tell it like it is and we won't try to blow smoke up your ass like we are the smartest guys in the room. We want you to understand and comprehend everything that we are explaining to you. Albert Einstein once said, "If you can't explain it simply, you don't understand it well enough yourself."

This book, of course, will be exactly like the two that have preceded it. I will dig deeper to save you time, money, and headaches. Not even the smallest expenses will be ignored (Beware the little expenses. A small leak will sink a great ship). I will discuss with you some more arguments that have occurred between ourselves and our tenants. Some tenants say that we are "ruthless ." We are not ruthless and if we find the tenants who are calling us ruthless, we shall destroy them!

We will prepare you so well that when you step foot onto the Section 8 housing field, you will be prepared to succeed. By failing to prepare, you are preparing to fail and that's where Nick and I come into the picture. We have seen it all and been through it all. You describe the scenario and we can tell you what kind of problem you're going to have, but more importantly, we'll tell you how to avoid that problem before it ever happens. You'll be like the lucky second mouse that comes along and inherits the cheese because the first mouse made a costly mistake. Nick and I are that first mouse. We made the mistakes and now we'll tell you how to avoid them. So, without any further ado, let's get it on!

CHAPTER 1

THE HIATUS

Many of you have asked a lot of questions over the last ten years so let's jump right in and get some of them answered, shall we? The main question, of course is, where have you been and are you still involved in Section 8 rentals? The answer to that is "yes," of course. Philly has kept their taxes very low and they have increased their fair market rents to about $1,100 for a three bedroom home, so it was a no brainer to stay involved. Ten years ago, we were only receiving $800 for a three bedroom and we thought we had it good then!

"Are you guys back up to the 300 home mark yet?" No, not quite. In fact, right now we are just a bit over the 125 mark. I'm in no rush to get there and we just simply move on the excellent deals now. Back in the day, we wanted every deal that came across our plate. We jumped at opportunities quicker than most people jump to conclusions. Once you make a little dough, you kind of put yourself in the driver's seat and you can pick and choose the deals that you want to make a move on. In time, I'm sure we'll get there, no rush.

"Do you guys still argue with your tenants?" Does a bear still shit in the woods? Of course! I'll probably argue with them until the day that I sell off my last Section 8 rental property, it keeps me young. It's been ten years and with an average of about 50 arguments and disagreements per year, that's about 500 more stories I've got to get too, so this is gonna be a lot of fun for you and I. Relax, I'll get to them.

"Do you guys still make mistakes?" Some, but not a whole hell of a lot. That's why it took me another ten years to write another book. In the early years, I couldn't stop making mistakes. I probably could have pumped out a book a month full of mistakes that I made. What an aggravating time. Sure I still learn from my mistakes, you're never too old to learn. I'll talk about a couple of mistakes I've made over the last ten years and what clever solutions we invented to correct them.

"Are there any new products that you guys can recommend?" You bet! Technology and manufacturing are changing every day and it's usually for the better. There are some things that I was doing ten years ago that I don't do now. There are some products that I was using back then that I'm not using now. There were products that were total shit back then but have improved themselves so significantly that I now use them in my rentals. I will talk about all of them in detail.

"Have you guys found anything else to eliminate?" Why yes, we have. What Nick and I do now is tear everything out of the property the minute we purchase it. We bring it to shell form. The kitchen cabinets get ripped out, the windows, the bathroom tub, vanity, toilet, etc, all gets ripped out. Then we proceed to Home Depot and purchase a bunk of ½ inch plywood which consists of 100 sheets. Then we cover everything in the property with the plywood. The walls, the ceilings, the floors, the windows, everything gets covered over in plywood. By the time we're finished, the entire house looks like a wooden box. Then, we rent it to a Section 8 tenant. We throw hay on the bathroom floor and come back about once a month to put fresh hay down. Of course, I'm kidding! See, I told you we were still nuts. The real answer is yes, we have found a couple more things to eliminate. Some we found on our own and some were sent in by other landlords. We will discuss all of them and why we decided to eliminate them.

"Are you still receiving tips from other landlords?" Yes! That's what I love about my website the most. At any given time, I can open up my email and find a plethora of emails from fellow landlords who have read my books and want to share their stories with me about a problem that they had and what they did to fix it. This book practically writes itself! All I have to do is put pen to paper. I will delve into some interesting landlord stories and tips.

"What has changed the most over the past ten years?" A lot, some for the good and some for the bad. Finding good tenants is one of the first things that pop into my mind on the bad side and rental increases are the first things that come to mind on the good side. Wow, I'm always thinking of money. Some things never change.

"Have you had to play dirty again?" I hate to admit it but yes, and I enjoy it every time! If someone is going out of their way to make my life miserable, I can't wait to turn the tables on them and make their life twice as difficult. I've got a gem for ya that pertain to lawyers, so in my book, that makes playing dirty twice as nice.

"Have there been any new rule changes?" Yes, and they always suck! As soon as you get used to doing something one way, Section 8 wants to change it up on you midstream because some idiot inspector decides that he has a safer way of doing something that has been around for fifty years. Anyway, I will discuss a few rule changes that pissed me off and what I had to do to correct them.

"Do you have any more street smart tips?" Sure, I'll throw in a couple of things to look out for, so you stay safe while working in the hood. One good thing is I haven't had to pull my gun out in ten years. Either I'm getting lucky or I've been around long enough that avoiding danger zones are now second nature to me. I still strap my gun on in the morning like I put my underwear on in the morning. In fact, if I had to forget one or the other, I'd pick the underwear. I feel safer with my gun!

The first two books were such a success that I'm going to stick to the script and use the same format. Eliminate, stories, landlord stories, landlord tips, and money saving tips will be the things that I talk about the most. How can you go wrong with that? I write my books with the same philosophy I use in life, "if it ain't broke, don't fix it." Now go open up a new bag of popcorn, get yourself comfortable, and enjoy Volume III.

CHAPTER 2

ANOTHER BALL BREAKING INSPECTOR

Well, since about 80 percent of my fan mail comes from people who love my stories, I won't keep the fan base waiting. I'll jump into a couple right off the bat. Okay, this story involves a ball breaking inspector, a new yet old product, and a big waste of my time and money. Like I've always said, I love a good story as much as the next guy but damn it, I hate being the punch line to the story. Here's what happened.

I was sitting in my rehabbed property, waiting for the inspector to shoot over, run through the property, and pass me. The place was sharp as a tack too. We bought it as a shell and put in a new kitchen, bathroom, plumbing, paint, etc. I signed a girl's three bedroom voucher a couple of weeks prior and now it was time for me to start getting paid for my sweat. That's when Fat Fu_walked through the door. This guy was about a tic-tac shy of 400 pounds and sweating profusely just from walking up the four front steps. I had never seen him before, and I knew I was in for a whole lot of fun. Miserable looking guy too, if he smiled his face would crack.

Although I hated to do it, I stuck my hand out to shake his. I figured I'd dry my hand off when he wasn't looking. Anyway, he shook my hand and it felt like I was shaking a dead fish, he had no grip whatsoever and his hand was just as I suspected, soaking wet. Don't know what this has to do with the story but that limp, sweaty grip is still etched in my brain, moving on. So now he starts inspecting the place. Everything went perfectly fine until the end of course. He walks over to one of the outlets and sticks his tester in it. I hear a "click" and in my head I say, "oh no."

"This outlet isn't grounded." I respond with, "It's the old 2 wire system that they wired the house with and it doesn't have a ground wire." "Well then you can't use these outlets, they all have to come out." I tried begging, I tried pleading, but Rerun wasn't having any of it. The minute he left, I tried calling the head of inspections, but he wasn't willing to put his ass on the line for a non grounded receptacle and I can't say that I blame him.

This outlet that had to come out

Ya see, the problem isn't the work that you have to do when you fail your initial inspection; it's the time and money that you lose. I had the receptacles replaced with the 2 prong with no grounding slot receptacles (I'll explain all of this 2 prong and not grounded stuff in a minute), two hours after the inspector left but now, I have to call back down to Section 8 and reschedule another inspection. If it takes a week for them to come back out and you are getting $1,000 a month for your rental, you just lost about $250 bucks. Also, you have a tenant who is chomping at the bit to get into the home and now, you have to call and inform her that the property failed inspection. It sucks and you run the risk of her backing out.

This is the outlet that had to be installed

Anyway, here's the deal. About five years ago a buddy of mine was working for an electrical supply house. They were going out of business and he grabbed me so many boxes of the 3 prong grounded receptacles that I had them stacked up to my asshole. I knew that using these outlets on a 2 wire system caused what is known as a "false ground" but hey, I got the receptacles for free, they were no more dangerous than what Section 8 wanted me to use and most importantly, they never stuck the tester in the outlets! I knew that the inspectors checked the GFI's to see if they were grounded, but never the receptacles. Until now that is.

I'll explain this as simple as I can to those of you who are not electricians. It's not very hard so follow along because this might come back to bite you in the ass like it did me. The rowhomes in Philly that I buy are about 80 years old and if I'm lucky, they have been updated through 3 phases of wiring. First, they started out with the old knob and tubing which is so obsolete that I won't even waste your time explaining it. From there, they moved to the 2 wire system which consists of a hot and a neutral wire (black and white), with no ground. From there, they moved to the romex wiring system which consists of a hot and a neutral wire (black and white), and a bare ground wire.

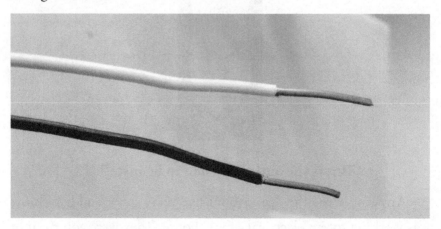

2 wire systems, notice no ground wire

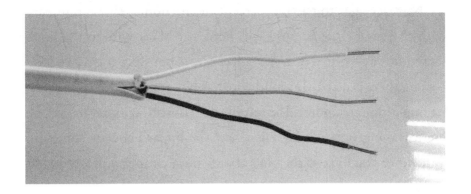

Romex system, with ground wire

I would say that 90 percent of the homes that I purchased had the newer romex wiring in place. For me, that's perfect when I'm switching out the old receptacles. I simply attach my black wire to the brass screw, my white wire to the silver screw, and my bare copper ground wire to the green screw. I'm done and the receptacle is grounded.

Romex wire connected properly with ground wire attached to ground screw

Now let's get to the ten percent of the homes that I purchase with the two wire system. I still hook my black wire to the brass screw and my white wire to the silver screw, but since it is a two wire system, there is no bare ground wire to hook to the green screw, thus leaving it nongrounded. The receptacle will still work perfectly fine but it is *not* grounded. Here is where the **hazard theory** comes in. Whenever you look at the plug of a vacuum cleaner or television, it looks like this.

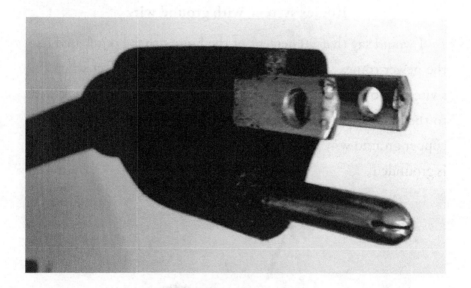

Vacuum cleaner cord

The vacuum cleaner cord has two prongs and a ground rod. The rod is the ground, so naturally if you plug into a receptacle that accepts the ground rod, you're going to assume that it is grounded but it is not because there is not a bare ground wire connected to the green screw inside the outlet. Therefore, the term "false ground" is used here.

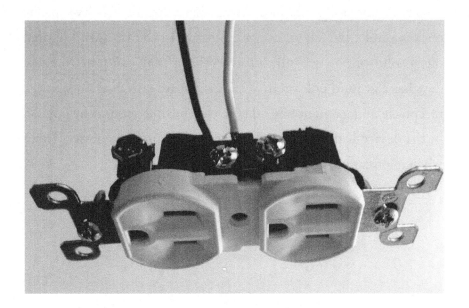

False ground. Notice that I can still hook up the hot and the neutral wire, which will power the outlet, but there is no ground wire to attach to the green screw to properly ground the outlet.

I still used my 3 prong outlets with the two wire system (until Fatso got a hold of me), because I have a ton of them and I was too cheap to go out and purchase the correct receptacles that you are supposed to use with the two wire system. If you have the two wire system, here is what you should use and it's real easy. They sell the old style outlet with two prongs and **no** ground pole slot. Simply hook up your black wire to your brass screw and your white wire up to your silver screw and you're done. There is no ground to hook up. You're not any safer using this outlet as opposed to the one that I was using. The only two differences is now, you know you are not grounded and the two prong outlets are way more expensive.

I have about eight homes where I have installed the two prong outlets and let me tell ya, they were a pain in the ass until I figured out a solution. Ya see, almost everything that you plug in these days has a ground pole on it. Well if there are only two slots on the receptacle and a tenant has a device that has the grounding pole on it, the device is not going to be able to plug into the outlet. That's when my freaking phone would ring!

Obviously this device has three prongs and the outlet only has two so it will not fit into the outlet.

"Hey Mr. Mike, I just moved in this place and I can't plug any of my stuff in ." What I started doing on move-in day was buying them about five adapters and showing them how to use them. After that, all has been fine thus far but give them about a year or so to lose the adapters and I'm sure my phone will ring again.

Adaptors I would give to my tenant on move in day.

This is how they work. The device plugs into the adapter and the outlet accepts the adaptor because it only has two prongs on it.

CHAPTER 3

LAWN BE GONE

It's survival in the city, when you live from day to day. Nothing grows and life ain't very pretty, when you're down that's where you'll stay. That's a line from a song called "In the City," by the Eagles and it isn't true! Unless I'm living in the wrong part of the city because the city where I'm investing in, everything F-in' grows. Front lawns, back lawns, trees, weeds, bushes, etc. Do you know how I know they grow? I know because I receive "nuisance fines" on everything that is unattended too and overgrown. Let me explain.

When I lease a home, I include in my lease that the tenant is responsible for all grass cutting and snow removal, no exceptions. That doesn't mean that they're going to cut the grass or shovel! In Philly, if you let your lawn get out of control, the city will issue you a "nuisance fine." It starts out at $50 and then goes to $75 and continues to climb from there until you pay it. I also have it written in my lease that the tenant is responsible for paying any and all nuisance fines. That don't mean they are going to pay them! Not until they are threatened, anyway.

For years I put up with two tenants, from April until October, every year that drove me nuts. One tenant wasn't too bad. I'd send her the citation; she'd pay it and cut the grass. The next month would roll around and it would be a carbon copy of the month that just passed, send her the citation, she pays and cuts the grass, all summer long with this bullshit. She was paying the fine so I kept my mouth shut.

The other tenant was just plain nuts. After the first nuisance fine for not cutting the grass was sent out to her, I got no response. I went over to her house in the middle of June and it looked like the jungles of Viet Nam. As I fought through the forest, also known as her front yard, to knock on her front door, I wondered, "How the hell lazy can you get?" When I knocked on the door, I found out that she was not only lazy, but also stupid. She referred to herself in the third person every two seconds. "Mrs. Rosie's coming to the door, Mrs. Rosie's tired, Mrs. Rosie doesn't cut any grass." When I informed her Mrs. Rosie's gonna be out on the street if Mrs. Rosie don't cut the grass and pay Mr. Mike his $50, she replies back, "Mrs. Rosie don't have no cutter." Uh, you fool, it's called a lawnmower and by the looks of this lawn, you'll also need a sickle. Keep in mind that this was not an old woman, we're talking about a 28-year-old girl. I would've had a little compassion if she was old but she wasn't.

Mrs. Rosie's yard

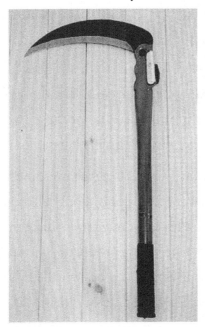

She'd need a sickle to cut it

By July, the lawn still hadn't been cut and she now had three outstanding fines on the property. They totaled $150. I pay the fines as they come in or it would have been a lot more. If I don't pay them, of course it will turn into a lien on my property, so I really have no other choice. Anyway, I ended up paying my lawyer $50 to dust her off a letter saying that if she didn't pay the $150 that she owed me, plus the $50 lawyer fee, she was going to be evicted and we would go to Section 8 to have her packet terminated. The good news is that she paid the money and cut the lawn. The bad news was that by the end of September, I was in the same boat again. The lawn was a mile high and she owed another $150 bucks. I called the lawyer, he sent her a letter, and the entire thing was straightened out again.

Both tenants played the same game with me for about seven summers. Believe it or not, for as lazy as they were, they kept their properties in good condition and I never had any problems passing my annual inspections. I guess I was lucky that both of their inspections were in January when no vegetation was growing. Still, this was pissing me off to no end. I almost hated the thought of summer rolling around because of these two idiots, and I love summer! Then a *good mistake* finally happed to me.

I went to Home Depot to purchase some weed killer for my own home. I just wanted to spray along where my sidewalk meets the street and where my driveway pavers meet my asphalt driveway. However, I grabbed the wrong product by mistake. What I grabbed instead of the weed killer was a product called Ortho Ground Clear. When I sprayed it along the curb and driveway, it only took about two days for the weeds to turn brown and die. What also happened was this shit ate into my lawn about a foot, killing the grass. It's that toxic that if it gets into the soil, it will kill everything in its path and nothing will grow there for the rest of the year. This stuff is more potent than Napalm! So I got an idea.

Ortho Ground Clear

It was still early spring so I grabbed a sprayer and mixed up my ground clear. I made it nice and strong, using 2 quarts per gallon of water rather than the one quart per gallon that it calls for on the mixing instructions. I drove up to Mrs. Rosie's house and started spraying her lawn like the Lawn Doctor fertilizes my lawn every year. The only difference was, he's feeding my lawn fertilizers and I'm feeding hers poison. After about five minutes of soaking her lawn in Napalm, here she comes barreling out the front door. "What're you doing to Mrs. Rosie's lawn?" I reply, "A favor." "What is that stuff?" I told her that it's a special spray that will slow the growth of the lawn down so she won't have to cut it so often (as if three times a year is often). Then, she thanked me and went back in the house. As soon as I finished, I drove around the corner and took care of the other lazy ass's lawn. Nick or I go back over about every six weeks too soak both of their lawns and I haven't received a nuisance fines since. The lawn looks like a brown carpet but I don't care, just as long as I don't receive any more fines.

Mrs. Rosie's lawn after using ground clear

The Ortho Ground Clear costs about $30 bucks for a two gallon jug but it is in concentrate form and it will last you all summer. Using a one gallon sprayer which costs about ten bucks and doubling up on the dosage, you'll be able to make four gallon sprayers full.

More than enough to kill any lazy tenant's lawn!

This is the $10 sprayer that I use.

CHAPTER 4

THE OLD LANDLORD WAS SHARP

Okay, I'm going to talk about filthy, disgusting roaches twice in this book. Not that I want too but I get so many questions on these dirty little S.O.B's that it would make your head spin. Some people say that God put everything on the face of this earth for a reason. Well if his reason for roaches were to annoy the hell out of landlords and cost them money, he did a fine job!

Disgusting roaches!

I would never exterminate while my tenant had possession of the property. However, I made damn sure that there was nothing walking around in the property before I gave the tenants possession of the property. If I just purchased a property or if a tenant had moved out and I was rehabbing the property, I did whatever it took to rid the property of any and all roaches. Once you clean out the property of all trash, food, etc, then clean, bomb and spray the property, the roaches will die or leave. They need a host to leave food out so that they don't starve to death. Combine no food and chemicals being sprayed all over the place and you rid yourself of any and all roach problems. Once the tenant takes possession of the property, it is now their responsibility to keep it roach free, and that's usually where your problem begins.

I owned a property that had just become vacant and the previous tenants were pigs. We cleaned out the property but still, the roaches were running wild, big suckers too. One was the size of an aircraft carrier with another roach riding on his back, no bullshit! We bombed and sprayed and came back the next day to do a body count. I had about a hundred of them upside down on their backs in the dining room and another two hundred dead on the kitchen floor, yet there were still a ton of them still walking around like they owned the joint.

I walked out to the truck to get my sprayer when I heard the old guy across the street yell, "Roaches huh?"

"Yep," I said.

"You're wasting your money with that stuff, that shit barely burns their eyes," he replied.

"Oh really, what do you have, secret roach repellant," I joked.

"No, but what I do have is a secret that will prevent you from seeing another roach in that house." Now he had me intrigued, I was all ears. "From day one, you have to prevent them from ever getting into your house to begin with and there is only one way to do it, Boric Acid. When you spray that spray of yours around, you kill half of them and the other half run under the walls, smoke a cigarette, and wait for the smoke to clear. You've got to keep them out from under the walls and there's only one way to do it, use the boric acid."

I had known that this old timer was a landlord up in the 'hood for years, way before I ever got up here. I said hello to him on a couple of occasions but after shooting the shit with him for about ten minutes, I was very impressed. He was 80 years old, still owned and maintained 18 homes, and was 200% upstairs. I think I'll have two marbles rolling around when I'm 80, yet this guy remembers who won the batting title in 1942 and what their average was. I don't know how some guys do it, but I will ask a favor of all my readers. If I'm still chasing Section 8 tenants and roaches around at age 80, please, hop on a flight to Philadelphia, take me out in a field, and put a bullet in back of my head. Thank you.

Anyway, I won't keep giving you the he said, I said end of it, but I will tell you exactly what he told me to do and it worked like a charm. It's very simple and it will make you scratch your head and say, "Geez, why didn't I think of that a long time ago?"

Hotshot Boric Acid

This procedure should be done when you first purchase a property or when someone moves out of one of your properties and you are rehabbing it for rent again. What's great about this tip is that you only have to do it once, and then you're good for years. First, you need to purchase Hot Shot roach killing powder with Boric Acid. Then, with a brick pointing tool or small putty knife, press the powder as far under the baseboards as you can get it. Do this throughout the entire house. Next, caulk between the baseboards and floor to seal the roach poison between the walls. You don't have to caulk the poison in, just pushing the poison behind the baseboards should be good enough but I go the extra mile by caulking and sealing it in.

Push the powder under the baseboards

This process establishes a boundary around your home that roaches will not cross. If they do, they will pick up the chemical with their feet, thus killing them. Typically, the roaches live and breed behind the walls of your property, but by sealing the walls off with caulk, you are preventing the roaches from getting behind the walls. Also, you are lacing the walls with poison which will kill the roaches. I didn't learn this tip until about eight years ago, so I've wasted many a dollar trying to kill the roaches that my tenants left me as a moving out gift. This has cut down on my roach problem tremendously. I'm not gonna say 100%, because some tenants are so disgusting that no matter what you do, you can't prevent them. But this tip has really been helpful and I've seen a huge difference when I get one of my properties back. When I talk about roaches again in Chapter 6, I'll tell you another thing I use to get them under control should your property become infested.

Pack the powder under the... hat bands

CHAPTER 5

THE BOYFRIEND

All of my stories are true and are always written with a purpose. If a tip, shortcut, product, or a way to save a buck is not attached to my story, I won't waste your time telling it. I've been in this crazy business for a long time and I have more stories than Walt Disney. I could write a million stories on things that tenants have said or done over the years but I won't waste your time if you're not going to learn something from it. In the next couple of chapters, I'll be discussing a few mistakes I've made over the past ten years. I'll also tell you how I corrected them. First, let's talk about mistakes.

There is one word that I hate more than the word mistake and that word is **"costly!"** Usually, "costly" is the word that appears before the word mistake, they go together like peanut butter and jelly. You rarely hear of anyone making a funny mistake or a nice mistake. No, they are usually costly mistakes. Whether a mistake is costing you time or money, they're no fun to make in this business or any other business that I know of. Even when I made a good mistake using Ortho Ground Clear, it cost me a couple feet of my lawn.

I've made a ton of mistakes and you'd think I would've learned everything by now but sometimes, you simply overlook a mistake and don't realize that you're making one until years later. They're the mistakes that I hate the most! Why? Because once I discovered that I had been making this certain mistake, I've probably already wasted thousands of dollars or hours of time by doing something the *wrong way.* Sure I will correct the mistake immediately but I will never be able to recoup that time or money that I have already wasted.

Thankfully, I don't really make a lot of mistakes anymore. As the old saying goes, "Don't find fault, find a remedy, anyone can complain." Well, they got the middle part right. I always find a remedy but I sure as hell, always find someone to blame and I usually complain a hell of a lot about the person I'm blaming. In this next case, it's the "boyfriend." Or should I say the dreaded boyfriend?

I can't tell you how many times my tenant's boyfriends have threatened to kick my ass, punch me in the face, or kill me. Hasn't happened yet, but I ain't getting any younger. The threats continued from the time I got into this business up until a few years ago when it finally hit me. Not my tenant's boyfriend's fist, but a remedy. A light bulb went off in my head one day that said, "it's your fault you idiot!" Let me explain.

I must have shown a property to a potential renter over a thousand times in my life, probably more. I'd say about half the time, the female tenant would be driven to the property by her boyfriend. I'd let them both in to check the property out and the majority of the time, the boyfriend would take the lead. "Are you going to put new carpet in here?" "What're you going to do about the washer and dryer hook-up?" "Can we paint?"

You know what I answered to all of these questions but even know I answered, "No, nothing, and are you crazy?" to his three questions, I was still making a big mistake which was, "WHAT THE HELL AM I DOING FIELDING QUESTIONS FROM THIS GUY FOR?" He plays no vital part in this scenario. He's not on the voucher yet he wants to run his mouth. For years, I put up with it because I simply wanted to get the house rented. The older I get the less patience I have for morons, so I cut it off at the pass and here is how I did it.

Now when somebody calls to see one of my rentals, I of course ask the usual questions. "Do you have a Section 8 voucher? Is it a two or three bedroom voucher? Do you have the voucher in your possession? When would you like to set up a showing?" But now, I also ask, "how many adults are on the voucher?" If she says that she is the only adult on the voucher, I tell her that when she comes to view the property, she and her children will be the only ones permitted to view the property. No boyfriends, no ex-husbands, no sisters, moms or dads. I will explain to her that it causes too much commotion and since she is the only adult on the lease, she will be the only adult that I will be dealing with, ever! If she doesn't agree to it, I simply move down the list and call the next tenant. Some will ask if it's okay for their boyfriend to drive them to the property, of which I reply, "Sure, just make sure he waits in the car or the showing is over."

I know it may sound a little harsh, but I've been roped into too many arguments with boyfriends who don't have any skin in the game. Believe me I've tried to give them a chance, Lord have I tried. Once they have their foot in the door and they have made their presence known, they think that you owe them the time of day and it never works out right. I'll give you a true scenario.

A woman and her boyfriend came to view and rented a three bedroom home from me. Two months later the toilet is clogged and of course my phone rings. It's the woman and she informs me that the toilet is clogged. I tell her to buy a plunger and plunge it. Then the bullshit starts! "Hold on, talk to my boyfriend." I swear to you never, and let me reiterate, **never** has any argument between myself, the tenant, and her boyfriend ended well. I must have been in a million of them and the boyfriend will take the girlfriends side every single time, so why argue with two assholes when you only have to argue with one? One will lie and the other one will swear to it, you'd have a better chance of winning an argument if you stood out back of your house and argued with a tree.

"Mr. Mike, this is Tyreek, Evette's boyfriend." Terrific, we're all on a first name basis now. "You've gotta come over here and unclog this toilet." "Tyreek, no I don't, read the clogged drain addendum attached to the lease Evette signed." "That don't matter, it was clogged when we moved in here." "Really," I said. "So for two months you've been using a toilet that's clogged?" "No," he says. "It just happened a couple of weeks after we moved in here." "Well there you have it, you clogged it, and you clear it, goodbye!"

If once, just once, a boyfriend would have sided with me, maybe I would have taken another phone call from one of them but they never did and I never will take one of their calls. I won't show them the house, I won't take their calls, and I don't even want to know that they exist. I'm sure that some of my tenants have a boyfriend living in their properties that are not on the lease and I don't care. Just as long as they never, ever have any interaction with me, I'm good. It's a lose/lose, proposition!

CHAPTER 6

ROACHES

If being hardheaded is a mistake, then I'm sure that I made a million of them! This mistake however, I think I corrected. In my early years, I'd argue with tenants until I was blue in the face about roaches. I wouldn't pay an exterminator to come out to their home for roaches, mice, or fleas no matter what. Hell, I wouldn't even pay for the cheese to go in the mouse trap. My theory was if they brought the roaches with them, they can either live with them or pay to get rid of them, it's their responsibility. I've softened my stand, just a little.

The number one thing that I hate about being a landlord is roaches. The second is fleas and I'm not talking about the tenants, real fleas. Sometimes a tenant can be so filthy that roaches will find their way into a property no matter what. I don't know if they walk across each others' backs to cross over the Borax poison that I use or what the deal is, but somehow they'll end up in one of my homes. When they do, one of two things is going to happen. Either the tenant or the inspector is going to call me. Then, the roaches become *my* problem.

A couple of years back, I'd argue with the filthy tenants who called me and would say, "The roaches weren't in the property when I rented it to you." They'd yell and scream back that I'm a slumlord and I don't want to do anything for them. A slumlord I am not, but they're right, I don't want to do anything when it involves me spending my money to fix a problem that they created. Behind every successful landlord stand 100 disgruntled tenants!

It makes zero sense to me that they can infest their homes with roaches to the point where the roaches are walking on the ceiling and then expect, let me correct that, demand that I pay an exterminator to correct their roach problem. I'll tell you this, if I so much as see an ant in my house, I'm tossing the cabinets of all open packages and spraying the hell out of the house. Not my tenants, they like to wait until the roaches carry the TV out the front door, it's disgusting.

Anyway, I've softened my stand on roaches a little bit. What I did was went out and purchased a $10 one gallon sprayer at Home Depot. Then I proceeded to Modern Exterminating, a local professional exterminating company in my area. I purchased a product called Master Line. It's 32 ounces and costs $40 but you can mix up and refill at least 16 sprayers full (using 2 ounces per gallon which is a strong mix). Now when a tenant calls for a roach problem I say, "I have the chemical mixed up in a sprayer. You're welcome to use it. I will swing back around your house tomorrow to pick up the sprayer when you have finished with it." Works like a charm and sometimes I even get a thank you out of them. Also, it is way cheaper than calling out an exterminator and way quicker than arguing with a tenant on the phone for an hour about why you're not doing anything about their roach problem.

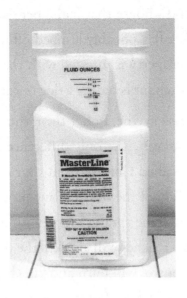

MasterLine Roach and Flea Spray

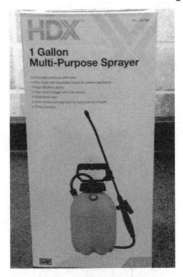

Again I use the HDX Home Depot Sprayer

Even know I don't permit pets, about once a year I will get a call from one or another of my tenants informing me that there are fleas in the property. Now I don't know, maybe one of their children had been visiting a friend's house that had a pet and they picked up a hitchhiking flea. The flea possibly jumped off in my property, laid eggs, and now my property is infested with them, it's possible. Or, I'm an idiot and my tenant is hiding a dog or cat in the basement.

Whatever the case maybe, I offer them the same solution; they are free to use my sprayer. The only difference is you will need to purchase a product called Gentrol from your exterminating store. Again, mix up a gallon of the Master Line product and throw one ounce of Gentrol into the sprayer along with it. The Master Line that you used for the roaches will also kill the fleas but it **won't** kill the flea eggs. The Gentrol will burn and kill the flea eggs. I tell the tenant to adjust the nozzle to fan spray and cover the carpets and floors with it when they are spraying for fleas. A one ounce bottle of Gentrol cost about six bucks.

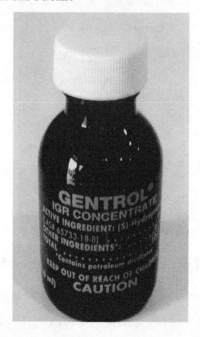

Gentrol for Flea Control

Mix it right in with the MasterLine

I must have that blood that the fleas love. If I walk into a home with shorts on and there are fleas in there, I'll know in about two seconds. About ten of them will jump on my legs and socks. I can't tell you how many times Nick and I left a property and then sat outside like two monkeys, picking the fleas off of each others legs. We learned a tip for this also, which I will pass onto you. An exterminator told us that the next time the problem of being covered in fleas arises, start up your truck or car and stick your foot about two inches away from the exhaust pipe. The fleas will jump off of you like I jump off the Philadelphia sports teams' bandwagon the minute they start losing. You don't want to get a flea in your vehicle and have it lay eggs.

Bottom line is this. For what equals out to a $3 sprayer full of roach juice, it's well worth it to avoid an argument with your tenant. Also, you totally avoid any fleas or roaches jumping on you. What I do is I pull up out front, call the tenant on the phone and tell them that I am here, come out front. I hand them the sprayer, tell them I'll be back the next day for it, and like a thief in the night, I'm gone!

CHAPTER 7

I PANICKED . . . AND MADE 3 MISTAKES!

About five years ago a landlord in the same area that we invest in, approached us about purchasing his six properties from him. Five of them were on very good blocks, in fact, I owned a couple of homes on the same street. One property however was on a block that Nick and I referred to as, "Ghetto Row." I really didn't want the property at all but it was more or less like an all or nothing ultimatum that he was giving us. I can't say that I blamed the guy. If we were to take the five good properties and leave him with the one piece of junk, he'd have no chance unloading it on its own. Anyway, the deal was so sweet on the package that it was almost like we were getting the property for free.

The property itself wasn't a piece of junk, in fact it was freshly rehabbed and looked very nice on the inside and out. The kitchen, bath, roof, heater, windows, etc., were all brand new. What made it a piece of junk was the block that it was on. About a third of the properties on the block were either boarded up or falling down. The other two thirds, excluding mine, were pretty shabby also. Ours was definitely the crown jewel of the block. Drug dealing, crime, and prostitution were known to be rampant on this block.

Was on this horrible block

This beautiful house

The block was full of board ups

I gotta stop and scratch my head when fellow landlords make an investment like this. Why on earth would you purchase a property on a block like this no matter how good the deal was? You're going to get the property cheap, then waste good money rehabbing it? Take the purchase money and the rehab money and go get a "not so nice" house on a good street rather than a nice house on ghetto row. Putting a new kitchen and bathroom into this joint was like putting earrings on a pig, I don't know why the hell he did it. Yet like an asshole, here I am buying the damn thing. Mistake #1.

After taking possession of the property and advertising it for rent, I barely got any phone calls or action on it. Prospective tenants saw what street it was on and just bypassed it like it was a bum on the corner begging for change. It appears that the tenants have more sense than me. I did get a couple of calls from people who had a two bedroom voucher, but this was a three bedroom home. I receive at least $1,050 per month for a three bedroom and I only receive $875 for a two bedroom home because that is all their voucher will cover. I bypassed the two bedroom voucher phone calls. Mistake #2.

After only receiving about seven or eight phone calls on the property (I usually get about 40 or 50 in the first week of listing a property), a guy calls me and says he needs to move right away. He told me he is *not* on Section 8, but he would give me $1,100 a month for rent and another $2,200 for security. He had a job and no prior evictions so I said, "Let's do it." Mistake #3

After showing the place eight times with no takers, I panicked. I felt as though I was racing against the clock. I'd better get this place rented soon before they break into it and I end up getting ripped off for copper and god knows what else. Let's face it; everyone on the street had to know it was a vacant rental the first time my white ass walked down the street to show it. Other than the mailman, I think that I was the only white guy to walk down that block in twenty years. I stood out like a piece of salt in a pepper shaker. So for the first time since "The Preacher" in Volume I ripped me off, I took a retail tenant and again, I paid the price!

Zero, that's exactly how much rent that I received from the guy after he took possession of the property, history had repeated itself. No police bailed me out by arresting the guy this time and I had to get him out the old fashion way which was eviction. By the time I paid for the eviction, lost four months rent, and rehabbed the place;

I was about three grand in the red after keeping his security deposit. Fool me once shame on you, fool me twice, I'm an asshole!

Finally after getting the property up and running again, I get a phone call again from someone with a two bedroom voucher. After the woman told me that she only had a two bedroom voucher, I was just about to hang up the phone when that damn lightbulb in my head went off again. It said, "Hey you greedy moron, stop waiting for that extra $200 bucks from a three bedroom voucher to roll in and get the damn thing rented." You can rent a tenant a 3 bedroom home if the tenant only has a 2 bedroom voucher but you're only going to get what their voucher maximizes out for, which in this case would be $850 as opposed to the $1,100 I would get if they had a 3 bedroom voucher.

Even at the $850 a month, I'm still cash flowing a couple hundred and the rent was now guaranteed because it was rented to a Section 8 tenant instead of to someone who wasn't on the Section 8 program. So I ended up renting the property to the woman with the 2 bedroom voucher. She felt as though she was getting a good deal because both of her sons could have their own bedroom and I was just relieved not to have to walk down that block anymore for showings. She has been in the home for the past five years; however, I have learned another thing that I don't like about owning shit holes. I fold up like a new suit when I'm threatened!

I find myself doing things for this woman that I wouldn't do for my greatest tenants. The first two years while I had her under lease, went perfectly fine. If she called me for something that was a tenant repair, such as a clogged drain or toilet, I'd inform her to read her lease and resolve the problem herself. After the two years were up and my lease became a month to month lease, the fun started. I tried to lock her up with another two year lease but she wasn't going for it.

A couple of weeks after approaching her about signing a new lease and being denied, she calls me for her carpets, which were brand new when she moved in, to be cleaned. I tell her that we don't do that and then she does the usual, complains! "It's Christmas time Mr. Mike and I'm having company over. Besides, if the carpets are getting cleaned, it's helping your property stay in shape." Gee, thanks for looking out for me and my property, you're a real sport. Anyway, I again tell her that I don't handle carpet cleaning and she says, "You don't do shit for me, I'm moving out of here after the holidays are over," and she hangs up on me. My asshole clinched up on me at the thought of trying to get that place rented again. "Uh oh," was the first thought that went through my mind. "Fix this," was the second thought.

The very thought of her moving out of there and having to drive down that street everyday while rehabbing the property made me sick. The thought of trying to get it rented again made me vomit, and the thought of **not** getting it rented made me come to my senses. For the very first time in my twenty plus years of being a landlord, I was in the carpet cleaning business. I waived the white flag and picked up the phone and called her back. I informed her that as a Christmas present to her and her family, I'd take care of the carpet cleaning. The reason that I told her it was a Christmas gift was so she would think that it was a one-time gift and hopefully she wouldn't think that her "moving out" threat had me chewing my nails off, which it did. I think that I was down to my knuckles. Anyway, she thanked me, told me she was staying, and now she had me by the balls!

She read right through my "Christmas Gift" bullshit like I was telling her Santa Claus existed. She wasn't buying it and has been a pain in my ass ever since. She always needs a gallon of touch up paint, I think she drinks it. I've cleaned the carpets—again, I've sent my guy over with the snake or the toilet plunger at least three times, and get this, I even hung a cheap screen door for her. I think that I've lost my mind! I'm in for about $700 bucks total over the past three years just to keep her happy and her ass planted there. However, if she moves out, I'm screwed so I have to bite the bullet on this one. You have to pick your battles and this is one that I'm not in a hurry to win. I may have spent $700 but I would have lost more with a vacant unit if she moved out on me. Do I like it? No, but it beats the alternative of the property not producing cash flow.

Had this property been on a nice block, I wouldn't have caved in. In fact, I would have told the tenant they were free to go after the lease expired, be my guest. But they don't go anywhere when it's a nice property on a nice block that they are living in. They know how hard these properties are to find. Once they know how good they've got it, they are the ones that cave in on their own threats and have to put up with me telling them what I'm **not** going to do for them, which is spend my money on things that I don't have to.

I'll tell you, this thing is not going to end well and if and when I write Volume 4, I'm sure that I will be including a story on how this thing ended. I'm sure it's going to escalate into her wanting a 24 hour maintenance man at her service or something crazy and I'm finally going to just throw the towel in with her. If and when push comes to shove, I already know what I'm doing with the property. Selling it! I don't enjoy being my tenant's human kick ball and I'm not going to go through this again. I got the property for next to nothing, made a couple of bucks off of it, so no matter what I get for it when I sell it, I'll be in the black. But for now, I'll continue to keep her in there just as long as the cash keeps flowing.

The moral of this story is please, do yourself a favor and don't invest on blocks like this. You're setting yourself up for failure and several things can happen, all of which are bad. You'll end up losing tons of rent money due to vacancy. You waste time and gas getting to and from showings that usually don't pan out. There's a good chance your property will be broken into and stripped of copper. There's a good chance you'll be robbed of your wallet walking down streets like this. And last but not least, you'll become your tenant's whipping boy. Since the first property was rented back in the Fred Flintstone era, the slogan best related to real estate still holds true today. Location, location, location!

CHAPTER 8

WOMAN ARE RIGHT, MEN ARE IMPOSSIBLE

Over the past twenty some years, I would say that we have rented about thirty of our homes to men with Section 8 vouchers. Every single time, I kicked myself in the ass and afterwards said, "What the F did you do that for?" Sometimes, you just want to get someone in the property so you can start getting paid on it and when someone comes along and says, "I'll take it," you sometimes throw caution into the wind and rent the unit.

Like I said, even though I've rented probably well over a thousand homes in my life, and only 30 were to men, I'd venture to say that half of my craziest arguments were with the male tenants. You see, woman want to yell and scream or try to jam you up with Section 8 when things go bad. Men, well they want to fist fight and threaten to kill you!

Nick and I both boxed a little in our younger years and if push came to shove when I was in my twenties, like an idiot, I might roll around in the street with ya for a little bit. One thing that I'm never going to do with a tenant of mine is lose my cool enough to go to blows. It's a no-win situation, for me anyway. If he knocks my teeth down my throat, I lose. If I knock his teeth down his throat, I still lose. He gets to sue me and Section 8 black balls me from ever renting another home in the Section 8 program. If I'm barred from the program, I won't have any more material to put together one of these fabulous books that you are reading. This is my livelihood and I'm not going to lose it for an idiot. I always remember two things a nun said to me back in the day when a fight broke out on the playground of my CCD class. She said, "Whatever begins in anger usually ends in shame" and "He who angers you, conquers you." My dad also gave me a religious one that said, "He who farts in church, sits in their own pew" but that one doesn't pertain to this story.

Well after renting a two bedroom home to a guy and his son, I left the lease signing saying, "Boy that guy's name sounds familiar." Anyway, he moves in and I don't hear a peep out of him for nearly a year, just the way I like it. The phone finally rings and he says, "Hey Mike, it's David. The annual inspection is coming up and I need you to come over and fix a lot of stuff so the house will pass inspection." Well first of all, the annual inspection was two days away and second of all I informed him, "That ain't how this works."

"Dave, the inspector tells me what to fix, not you."

He returns, "Yeah, but I got a lot of stuff I want done too."

I must have been bored and just to humor myself, I ask, "Like what?"

"Well my son's bedroom door fell off the hinges (impossible, had to be knocked off). Two cabinet doors are broken (when I got there, they were splintered like Kung Fu was practicing his karate). The kitchen sink is clogged (I don't do clogs). Two smoke detectors are beeping (change the batteries you idiot). Two stove knobs are missing (find them). And I'd like you to paint my son's room." (Now, I'm speechless)!

I ask him, "Are you F-in' kidding me? You're destroying my house like a human wrecking ball and you think that I'm going to reward you with a paint job, seriously?" I ask.

He returns, "You ain't gotta be disrespectful like that, I'm coming at you like a man." Uh, what the hell does that mean?

I said, "You're coming at me like an idiot. Everything you mentioned is a tenant repair and I'm not fixing any of it and I'm not painting anything."

Again he returns with more of the hard guy bullshit that I don't even comprehend. "You ain't gonna disrespect me, the last guy that disrespected me got his cap peeled." "Whatever dude, I'll see you in two days," I said.

Two days roll around and I meet the inspector in front of Dave's house, I knew this was going to be a lot of fun. As soon as we stepped foot in the living room, I now know why his name sounded so familiar. I used to watch a ton of boxing back in the 80's and early 90's. On the living room wall hung a giant championship boxing belt. Next to the belt was a huge picture of this idiot in the ring with the referee holding his hand up as the winner of the fight. His name sounded so familiar to me because at one time, he was a well-known Philadelphia fighter. Look, I'd rather jack a lion off with a handful of roofing nails instead of fighting this guy to begin with, but now knowing who he was made me even more uncomfortable. He must have fallen on bad times and I thought in my head, "What great luck you have Mike, you probably picked the only heavyweight boxer in the world on Section 8 to rent to. Maybe you could see if Mike Tyson wanted to rent your vacant house around the corner while you're at it."

Future tenant?

Let's proceed with the inspection, shall we. The first thing we get to is the kitchen and there are the splintered cabinet doors. When I asked him what the hell happened to them, he says, "You ain't gotta talk disrespectful to me." Here we go again with this respect bullshit.

I said, "But it's okay for you to disrespect my property?"

That's when the inspector jumped in and it was all downhill from there. "Mike, don't worry, I got you. I'm writing it up as a tenant repair."

Dave chimes in with, "What's that mean?"

"It means you have to fix it," I said.

"Shut up Mike, I'm talking to the inspector." After the inspector tells him the same thing that I just told him, he now wants to fight the both of us! "You two had this shit planned, I saw you talking out front. This shit keeps up, I'm gonna take both ya'll out front!"

I know I've still got my ace in the hole strapped to my side, but this guy was one big dude, not to mention he made a living caving people's skulls in. I'd probably have to hit him with all six bullets and then throw the gun at him just to get out the door. The inspector didn't like the direction that this thing was going in either. You could feel it escalating from the time we walked in the door. I'm sure the inspector seeing the champ's boxing picture and belt hanging on the wall helped him make his next decision really easy. "I'm stopping this inspection right now. You just threatened me."

Dave's tune changed in a hurry. "No, I didn't sir, I threatened Mike." Gee, thanks pal.

The inspector wasn't backing down and I give him credit. "No, no, you threatened both of us and I'm going to report this incident to your service rep and let her handle it from there. We will have to reschedule this inspection."

Dave could see the handwriting on the wall and he instantly went into the begging and pleading mode. "Please mister, just work with me. Don't report me, I'm sorry. I can't lose that voucher; me and my son don't have anywhere to go if I get kicked off."

The inspector stuck to his guns and ended the inspection. As Dave walked out front with us, I could see he wanted to kill the both of us but he kept his composure, thank god!

I got in my truck, the inspector got in his car, and we both drove away. When we got around the corner, I blew my horn for him to pull over. We got out of our vehicles and both asked each other almost simultaneously, "Did you see the belt and picture on the wall?" We both had a good laugh but I'm not going to lie, that was scary and I don't want to be put in that situation again.

Still, I had the problem of, "what am I going to do with this maniac that's living in my house?" I know that after the inspector reports him, they are going to throw him off the program and I'm now going to be stuck getting rid of him. Anyway, I took a risk and it worked.

I was pretty good friends with the inspector and I asked him if he could hold off on reporting the incident. He asked me why and I told him that I had a plan to get this guy out of my house, quickly. He said he'd hold off for a day and mark it down as a "could not enter." What I did was I drove back over to Dave's house and asked him if he could come outside, we have to talk (I really need my head examined). Right away, he wanted to get up in my face and I told him, you can either hear me out or you're going to lose your voucher. He chose option A. I told him that the inspector was going to have his voucher squashed because of the threat that he made against him.

I said, "If you go down and get an emergency packet to vacate my house, I'll talk the inspector out of filing the threat claim on you."

For him, it was a win, win. He no longer had to deal with me and he got to keep his voucher (I did keep $900 of his security). For me, it was also a win, win. I got rid of an asshole and didn't have to go through a long, drawn out eviction. Oh, and I also didn't get my cap peeled, so that was good too. For the record, I later found out that the, "peeling of the cap" means someone shooting you in the head, nice huh?

My solution to this entire scenario is very, very, easy. I no longer rent to men, plain and simple! I've always felt a little odd doing it anyhow. If you're a man, have a family and your health, why shouldn't you work? Rarely, nothing ends well and when you're renting your property to a guy on Section 8, it definitely won't end well. I'm a numbers guy and I always play the odds. Out of the thirty homes that I've rented to men, I've argued with each and every one of them at one time or another. I've come to the conclusion that if it has tires or testicles, sooner or later you're going to have trouble with it.

I've had beautiful landlord-tenant relationships with about 80% of my tenants, all females! I know you wouldn't know it from my stories but like I always say, I don't have stories to tell about the good tenants. You are setting yourself up for failure or a fist fight when you rent to men. Play the odds and stick to renting your properties to woman, the arguments will end civilized, like in court rather than the hospital or the city morgue.

CHAPTER 9

COPPER IS THE NEW "GHETTO GOLD"

In the next five chapters, I will be discussing some of the new, great products that have hit the market over the past ten years. These products have either saved me a fortune or made my life a hell of a lot easier. The first one that I will be talking about is called "Pex" and it has done both! Let me tell you, when I first started out in this business twenty something years ago, I **never, ever** had the copper from my property ripped off. Now, it's an epidemic. Thank god for Pex, but first I've got some stories to tell.

The first time that I got ripped off! We hadn't even been in the business for a year when I had my first encounter with a scrap thief. I remember it like it was yesterday. It was a cold, rainy, Sunday morning. I wanted to get up to the property, do what we had to do, and get back home in time for Eagles kickoff (maybe a little earlier so I could get some bets in). Anyway, as we were driving up the street, a guy goes walking past us with a shopping cart full of scrap. Downspouts, cans, a bike, a screen door, you name it and if it was metal, it was in his cart. Whatever he could pry off the houses with his bare hands, I guess. After we pass him Nick says, "I'm gonna go back around the block again, I think that asshole has our screen door on his cart." This was before we started eliminating screen doors, now he would have been doing me a favor. I told Nick that he was wrong because the house that we were working on didn't have a screen door. He says, "Not the one we are working on, the one around the corner. I'll know because it has a sticker of the American flag on it." We go back around the corner and sure as shit, the door has the flag sticker on it.

Rage flew through both of our bodies and we both jumped out of the truck. "Hey asshole," Nick shouted, "That's my screen door!" Most people would have said that they found it and you can have it back. Not this guy, and mind you, I wasn't licensed to carry yet so I didn't have my gun. The scrap thief returns, "No mother effers, this is my door," as he reaches into his waistband and pulls out a big, rusty steak knife that if it didn't kill me by penetration, I'd probably die of lockjaw from the rust on it. We didn't so much as have a baseball bat in the truck to thump his skull in with and we didn't have a cell phone to call the police with because cell phones were a thing of the future back in the early nineties.

Now, it was like a Mexican standoff (is that politically correct these days? I don't know). He wasn't taking the door out of the cart and we weren't ready to let him scrap our door. Finally, he said that if we didn't get out of his way, he was going to start cutting. Nick said, "Fair enough," and told me to get back in the truck. Once we were both in the truck, Nick floors the truck at him and the cart! He jumped one way and the cart full of shit got smashed the other way. The door landed about ten feet away from him and I jumped out of the truck and threw the door back on the truck. Nick threw the truck in reverse and dared him to get back into the street, but he declined.

The anger that ate at both of us was off the charts. I don't install storm doors anymore but if I had to, that would have set me back at least a hundred bucks. All that the bum is going to get at the scrap yard for the damn thing is five bucks and that's what burns me up even more. It's even worse with copper! These guys will try like hell to break into your property (I've got a lot more tips to prevent break-ins too), and if they get in, they'll strip every piece of copper in the joint. They'll get about a hundred bucks at the scrap yard, meanwhile, if you don't know what you're doing, you might end up paying a plumber $2,500 or better to replace the copper. Finally, someone invented something that a scrapper won't ever touch and it's called "PEX!" What a wonderful invention and so, so easy to use. Instead of using expensive copper that can be scrapped for your water supply lines, you are now using inexpensive plastic that has no monetary value to a scrapper. You can by a 300 foot spool of it for $85 bucks and the only other things that you'll need is the Pex crimp tool and the fittings. The crimping tool cost about $60 bucks. Simply watch a couple of YouTube videos on how to use Pex and you'll be an expert in an hour. I kid you not, it's like tying hoses together, it's that simple!

Spool of Pex

Pex Crimping tool

Let me save you another $175 bucks right off the bat, because that's what I do. All the YouTube videos will show you and tell you that you need to use a "Pex manabloc" or "Pex manifold." What the manabloc does is, picture your electric breaker box with each separate breaker being able to turn on and off a single appliance, such as your stove, microwave, heater, or air conditioning. Well a manabloc does the same thing, only with water. From the manabloc, you will be able to separately turn off your washer, water heater, or your kitchen sink, etc.

Here's how I'm going to save you the cash. You don't need a manabloc! Not for a rental property anyway. The guy at the plumbing supply house or Home Depot will try to offer it to you but tell them no thanks. Sure if it were being installed in your home, you 'd like the luxury of being able to separately turn off hose bibs, toilets, or whatever may be leaking in the home until you get it fixed, but in a rental property, you don't need to.

Pex Manibloc. Unnecessary.

Simply bypass the manabloc and run your line directly into the main ball valve. If you need to turn off the water to any fixture in the house, simply turn your main ball valve off and it will shut the water down in the entire home. Repair your problem or leak, turn the ball valve back on again and you're in business. People have lived for hundreds of years without a manabloc and if I live for another hundred years, my tenants will also live without a manabloc.

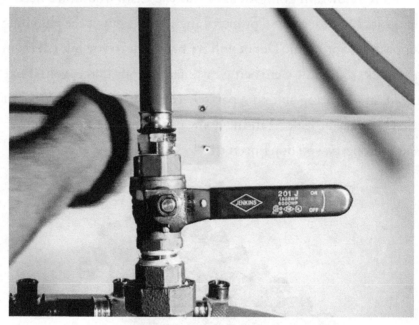

Bypass the Manibloc

I'm telling you, without a doubt this product has simply made my life a hundred times easier! By far and away, Pex is the greatest money saver that I have ever come across. It kills three birds with one stone. First, it's cheaper than copper. Second, it's easier to use than copper. And third, thieves leave it alone! It's like leaving a steak out for a vegan; they're not going to touch it!

CHAPTER 10

BEHR PAINT, MOST IMPROVED PLAYER

Earlier in both Volume I and Volume II, I talked about a paint called MAB and how wonderful it was. Notice how I say, **"Was."** Since Sherman Williams took them over, this paint has lost its luster and has gone downhill faster than a wagon full of fat kids. What's worse is it has nearly doubled in price. It's half as good as it once was and twice the price, that don't sound good.

If you remember correctly, I told you that I was purchasing their primer and simply painting with that. The walls would come out the color of bone white paint and I rarely needed two coats. My tenants couldn't tell the difference, so they loved it, I saved cash so I loved it, and we both would have lived happily ever after if Mr. Sherman Williams never came along.

Shortly after their take over, I began to see a sharp increase in their pricing. When I asked why I could no longer get a five gallon bucket of primer for $18 bucks, the manager replied, "We are under new ownership." Soon, the paint went from $18 for a bucket of primer to almost $60. Not only that, it wasn't even covering like it normally did. So when I complained about that also, I was told the EPA had them take a couple of chemicals and pigments out of the paint. Whatever they took the hell out, must have been the stuff that made the paint good in the first place because now, it sucks. It was taking me two or three coats just to cover the walls.

I had already used every paint under the sun, MAB, Behr, Glidden, Finnaren & Haley, ect. All the ones that I just mentioned always took at least two coats so I figured if I was going to paint with junk (because that was all that was out there), I may as well paint with the least expensive junk and that is when I hit the jackpot with my new discovery!

I went to Home Depot to grab a five gallon bucket of Behr paint. Their product was shit but now, so was MAB's and Behr was cheaper. As I looked at their products, I see a label that says, "Guaranteed to cover in one coat." My bullshit detector went off but I figured I might as well try it because I have nothing to lose at this point. The five gallon bucket seemed a lot heavier to me than that of MAB's five. Anyway, I took it back to the property and decided to give it a whirl myself. As I poured it out, it seemed very, very thick and as I rolled it on to the walls, it was covering everything. Dirt, water stains, old paint, roach shit, everything! I finally had to stop and read the label to see what the hell was in this paint. Two seconds into reading the label, I got myself sick.

The label said, "2 in 1 paint ." What the hell is that, I thought? As I read further, it simply means that they actually put the primer right in with the paint. Why was I sick you ask? Because I had been doing this for years! If a property was really bad, I'd cut a half of a five gallon bucket of white paint with a half of a five gallon bucket of primer and wha-lah! The paint would cover beautifully and had I known you could patent and manufacture this type of paint, I would have come out with my own brand of paint, sold off all of my rentals and moved to an island. I'm not acting like I'm the Christopher Columbus of my painting discovery because I'm sure there are thousands of other painters who knew of this trick before I was even born. But none of us had the sense to take the product to market so there for, I'm still stuck in this same Section 8 rental game with you.

I'll let Behr off the hook for stealing my idea because they really put together a great product and it does cover in one coat just like the label said it would. I use the Behr Premium Plus which goes for $108 for a five gallon bucket and is the cheapest in their product line. There is nothing that I hate worse than rolling out an entire property and than realizing that everything is bleeding through and I have to roll the property out again. Time is money and only having to roll once saves me a lot of it!

Behr paint. Most improved player!

CHAPTER 11

10 YEAR SMOKE DETECTOR

Over the past twenty years, I imagine I've owned over 500 homes. I'll ballpark it and say that I installed six smoke detectors in each home (basement, first floor, hallway, and three bedrooms). That comes out to a total of 3,000 smoke detectors. That number alone sounds high but here is where I start to get nauseous.

In twenty years, I've probably turned each of the homes over at least three times. What I mean by "turned over" is during my ownership of the property, a tenant will move out and I will retake possession of the property and I'll have to rehab it again to get it up to snuff to pass the next Section 8 initial inspection. What I find 90% of the time is that I have to change all of the smoke detectors again. Why? Because they are either missing or broken!

**Tenants love to store smoke detectors in the kitchen
drawer rather than simply changing the batteries.**

Here is what happens. If a smoke detector in my home or your home starts to chirp or beep, we obviously change the battery. What do the tenants do? Well let's see. If they have a ladder or a chair nearby, they stand on it and remove the smoke detector from its bracket. But instead of changing the battery and re-hanging the smoke detector, they remove the battery and throw the smoke detector in the bedroom closet, a kitchen drawer, or in the trash. When you ask them where the hell it got too, they tell you that it was broken because it kept beeping so they threw it in the trash. When you tell them that the beeping is an indicator to change the batteries, you usually will get, "Ya'll didn't give me no extra batteries." A mind is like a parachute, it doesn't work if it's not opened.

Okay, you were lucky if they had a ladder and took the smoke detector down properly. There's a slim chance that they could find it in a bedroom drawer, under the bed, or whereever, but most of the time, if it were wedged up their ass sideways they can't find it. If you do hit the lottery and find it, you would than change the battery and save a couple of bucks. However, if you weren't lucky and they didn't have a ladder, they usually just smash the smoke detector from the bracket with a broom handle and snap the tit on the bracket. Now you're forced to purchase an entire new smoke detector because the smoke detector companies are not stupid. They are smart enough to make you purchase the entire smoke detector; they don't sell the brackets separately. When I watch the news at night and see a fire where five or six people were killed and the newsman says, "None of the smoke detectors were working properly," I think to myself, what morons!

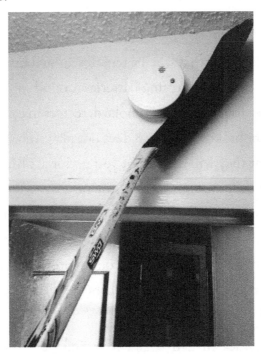

Smoke detector or hockey puck?

Broken tit on smoke detector bracket

It got to the point that when a tenant's annual inspection rolled around, I was not only carrying batteries around in my truck with me, I was also carrying a case of smoke detectors in case any of them were missing or broken. Section 8 does not play around on this! The first thing that they will do is right you up for a 24-hour violation, meaning that they are coming back the next day to make sure that the smoke detectors are working properly or you won't be getting paid. It makes no sense to me why **you** fail the inspection if the tenant does not want to put 99 cents out to protect his or her family but the system is ass backwards sometimes and lacks accountability. Anyway, back to my math problem.

So 500 homes turned over three times each, equals 1,500 turnovers. Six smoke detectors put in each time equal nine thousand

(1500 x 6 = 9,000). Add in about another 2,000 smoke detectors that I have changed during annual inspections and that comes to about 11,000 smoke detectors that I've purchased in my life. At about six bucks a clip that comes out to a cool $66,000 in smoke detectors alone! I could be driving around in a brand-new Corvette but instead, I have my money invested in smoke detectors. Wow, now I'm beyond nauseous. Wish I didn't do the math.

Kidde Code One ten year smoke detector

Well now, that problem is solved. They finally came out with the answer to my smoke detector prayers. The Kidde Code One sealed 9 volt, ten year lithium battery smoke detector has arrived! What it is is simply a smoke detector in which the battery is sealed within the unit and will last for ten years. You no longer have to worry about your tenant using the smoke detector as a hockey puck when it starts chirping because it won't chirp for ten years, guaranteed. No more broken brackets, no more "missing" smoke detectors, and no more 24 hour smoke detector violations. They are more expensive than the cheap smoke detectors, but you'll save time and money by not having to replace them, headaches not having to look for them, you'll pass your inspections, and most importantly, you'll keep your sanity from not wanting to kill your tenant.

On a quick note, the Kidde Smoke Detector lists at $14.99. I have found them as low as $11 bucks and, this is where I get nuts, I called Kidde and asked if I could get a deal on a bulk shipment. I purchased 200 of them and they shipped for free. I was able to get the price down to just north of $8 bucks.

CHAPTER 12

NEW LOCKS – LESS HEADACHES

A couple of years back, we were using the Kwik-Set, double pack locks. They are still an outstanding lock which even today, I have installed on my home. They came with 2 doorknobs, 2 deadbolts, and 4 sets of keys. Throw a set on the front door, throw a set on the back door, hand your tenant 2 copies of the keys on move in day, and you were done. If it would've continued like that, of course I wouldn't be writing this fun and exciting chapter.

Kwik Set double pack

Before I tell you what we use today, let me tell you that some tenants are put on this earth, solely to break my balls. Usually they are already living in my property before I find out that they are ball breakers but on this occasion, I was lucky enough to figure out that she was a stone breaker before she ever took possession of the property. I could see trouble coming down the street like a taxi coming down Broadway.

"Move in day" is usually ass kissing day for you and your tenant. They promise you how much they're going to take good care of your property and you won't have any problems with them. You shake their hand, wish them well, hand them two copies of the keys and you're on your way. Not this time! Now I've had a tenant or fifty, ask me for an extra key but this woman was insane. My usual response to, "Can I get a couple extra keys?" is of course not and you can go to Home Depot and they'll make you as many as you want. I only provide 2 sets of keys. Every other tenant I had told to get their own keys made up was okay with it and didn't have a problem, but this woman didn't want one extra key, she wanted six. Here's the story.

I had already received a bad vibe in my gut with her when we were signing the leases at the Section 8 office. She wanted to know why there was a check mark in the box that said, "No schedule" on exterminating. I replied, "Because I don't do exterminating." She replies back, "What, I'm supposed to get rid of your roaches?" I say, "No, you're supposed to clean up after yourself and you won't have a roach problem." Fair enough, right? She shook her head, rolled her eyes, and reluctantly signed the lease. We both leave the Section 8 office and I tell her that I will meet her at the property in a half hour, and here is where the fun starts. "Make sure it's a half hour, I got shit to do," she says. Uh, okay boss.

I drive slower than usual to just to break 'em for her and when I pull up, she is already there and sitting on the front steps of the property. I'm halfway out of my truck and I didn't even get a chance to scratch my ass yet and she yells, "You gonna give me a bunch of keys right?" Um, what? As I approach her, I tell her I'm giving her two copies of the keys and if she wants more, Home Depot is around the corner. "I need six extra sets. All my children need a key, my boyfriend needs a key, and my Mom needs a key."

First of all, she has kids that are four and six years old on the lease. Second of all, her Mom and her boyfriend are not even on the lease. I calmly reply back, "Again, you are only getting two sets of keys." "This is bullshit, my last landlord gave me as many as I wanted, he wasn't cheap like you!" I feel like I'm dealing with aliens sometimes. I'm about an hour into our beautiful landlord-tenant relationship and I'm already three arguments deep with this nut. She hasn't even stepped over the threshold of the door yet and she's running her mouth at me like I'm her chump. That's when she got the other side.

"How about this, I'm not giving you one F-ing key because you're not moving in my house." "Too late, I already signed the lease," she snapped back. "No, you don't get it. The lease doesn't mean shit until you take possession of the property and I'm not giving you possession. I know a pain in the ass when I see one and lady and you might be the biggest one I've ever come across."

I'll spare you the rest of the argument and the unpleasantries that were exchanged between the two of us but she never did take possession of the home. What she did do for me was set the wheels in motion to find a different type of lock to use. I had grown tired of the tenants losing both sets of keys and calling me up and asking me if I could make them a spare. Even know they were paying for it, it was still a hassle. Finally, I found my solution!

We now use the Schlage Camelot keypad deadbolt lock and they retail for $84 bucks. These are the best things that have hit the market in a while. When my tenant moves into the property,

I program two codes into the lock for them to use, one code for themselves and one for a guest if they want to give it to them. I also program my landlord code (this is my master code that I program into all of my locks), so I never have to carry any keys around with me anymore. The tenant will never be able to change the codes because you need a *programming code* to do it, which only I know because I'm the one who programs the code in. It's real simple, trust me, and the lock comes with a lifetime guarantee.

Keypad Deadbolt

Schlage Camelot Lock

The only down feature about the lock is that it does operate on a 9 volt battery. I use a lithium battery and I can get about four years out of them, however, I will change the battery every two years during the tenant's annual inspection and I have had zero dead battery issues so far, knock on wood! The reason that the battery last so long on this lock as opposed to the Kwik-set keyless lock is that once you enter the code to open the door, you still have to manually turn the unlock knob. With the Kwik-set keyless lock, once you enter the code, the batteries automatically turn the deadbolt and open the door. I used the Kwik-set at first, but it was costing me a fortune in batteries due to the automatic feature. It used 4 AA batteries and they went dead on me about twice a year. The Schlage is the way to go, it really is a great lock and they have some easy "how to videos" on YouTube on how to install and program this thing.

They cost $84 but they're worth their weight in gold! Here are some of the advantages.

1. I don't have to make copies of keys anymore.

2. When the tenants move out, I don't have to change the locks anymore, I simply change the code.

3. No more lock-outs. I never came over to one of my properties to rescue a tenant from being locked out anyway, but now you don't even have to put up the argument on "why you're not coming out."

4. You don't have to carry keys around with you anymore and you don't have to carry around a book with individual passage codes to each property in it. Program your land-lord master code into every lock, keep the code the same and you'll be able to get into every property, every time.

5. No more broken keys! I've had at least twenty incidents where the tenant's key got old and weak and ended up snapping off in the lock. If your lucky, you get the broken key out with a pair of needle nose pliers. If you're not lucky, you're changing the lock.

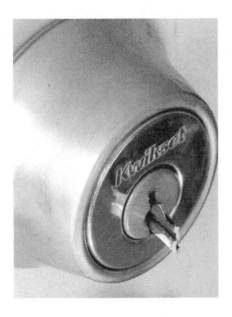

No more broken key problems

This lock will save you time and money of course, but it will save you numerous arguments with your tenants about copies of keys, lost keys, broken keys, and lock-outs!

CHAPTER 13

VULKEM SEALANT 116

Back in Volume 2, I told you that we were using a product called "Vinyl Patch" to repair cracks in our sidewalks. Although vinyl patch is a great product, we found something even better to use. Not only is it better, it's also cheaper and easier to use than vinyl patch!

The product is called Vulkem Sealant and what it basically is, is concrete patch in a caulking tube. Instead of mixing up the vinyl patch in a mixing pan, getting my hands and tools dirty and then having to clean the tools and the pan out again when I've finished, now I simply load a tube of Vulkem Sealant into my caulk gun, cut the tip to open it, and then go to town caulking any and all cracks on my sidewalk so I don't fail inspection.

Vulkem Sealant, 30 ounce tube, self leveling

Easily loads in caulk-gun

Before

This stuff is even better than the vinyl patch because it's flexible and water repellant. It will form a tight, water proof seal on any crack. It's self leveling, mold and mildew resistant, and comes in different colors so you can match it up to your sidewalk. The vinyl patch had a gray finish and would stick out like a sore thumb on white concrete.

The feature that I like best about it is its flexibility. It gives you excellent performance in moving joints. What this means is usually when you get a crack in the sidewalk, it's from settlement. One side of your block will drop down a half inch and the other side will stay put. Something has got to give and you usually will get a crack right down the middle of your block.

When we patched these cracks with vinyl patch, the patch would hold up for a year or so but the minute that block dropped another half inch on one side, the vinyl patch would now crack and I'd be out there taping the sidewalk back together for the next inspection. With Vulkem, you don't get that. This stuff expands and moves with the crack. It works great on any concrete surface and costs about $7 bucks for a 10.1 ounce tube. However, I use the jumbo 30 ounce tube so I don't have to keep reloading the caulk gun and of course, it's cheaper. The 30 ounce tube costs $14 bucks but you get three times as much.

After

The only complaint that I have about this product is that if you get this shit on your hands, it's hard as hell to get off. I'm Mr. Clean and I hate to go into a store, reach out for change, and have crap all over my hands. I've had the best success in removing this stuff from my hands with WD-40 but it's still a battle if you don't get to it before it dries. Wear gloves while you're applying it and you won't have any complaints. I'm usually in to much of a rush to go back to the shop and grab a pair of gloves so it's my own fault. If you have used this product and know the ancient secret of removing it from your hands, drop me an email and I'll get you in the next book.

CHAPTER 14

PREVENTING BREAK INS

In Volume 1, chapter 13, I wrote about securing your property while vacant. To this day, I still use every one of the tips and precautions that I talked about back then. The good news is that I have found a pretty inexpensive way from even being attempted to being broken into. I just talked about copper theft becoming an epidemic over the years and I knew that I had to do more to combat it. I knew that if I really put my mind to it, I'd come up with something more to add to my repertoire. So, I did!

Here is my theory. Two guys come walking down the street and you have to fight one of them. The guy on the left is 5 foot 6, not built at all, and weighs 150 pounds soaking wet. The guy on the right is 6 foot 2, built like The Rock, and weighs 250. Who are you going to pick to fight? You'll pick the guy on the left of course, unless you have a mental illness. It's the *physical appearance* that makes you not want to fight the big guy.

Unfortunately, that "physical appearance" luxury doesn't come into play when you're talking about rental properties. Or does it? If there are two vacant properties on a block, which one is a thief going to try to break into? Probably both, but he will first try to break into the one that appears to be the easiest target and also has the safest exit strategy. So my thought was this, if all the properties on the block look the same, how can I make my property appear more intimidating? I had to think of something that would intimidate a thief enough to make him back down and walk away from my property before he even attempted to break into it.

The solution to the problem was cameras! You all know me to well by now to know that I am not going to go out and purchase a Smart Surveillance Camera System, which costs about $150, for a rental property. What I did was jump on Amazon and searched, "Dummy Camera." There are a ton of them on there and they are all fairly cheap. The ones that I like to use are the Idaodan Dummy Security cameras. They cost $19.99 for a pack of four of them. That's only five bucks a camera!

Idaodan dummy camera

I like using these cameras as opposed to the Wali Dome dummy cameras, which cost about the same but are less intimidating looking than the Idaodan cameras. A thief, if he is not looking up, may not see the Wali Dome camera but he'll sure as shit see the Idaodan camera, they stick out like a giraffe driving a Volkswagen.

The minute we purchase a new property or one of my rentals become vacant, I shoot over to the property and install 4 fake cameras, 2 in the front and 2 in the back. I like to mount them up high where a kid won't throw a rock at them and a neighbor or thief won't try to steal one of them. They are easy to mount and should only take you about fifteen minutes. It will be the best fifteen minutes of your time that you ever spent! The camera has a flashing red light in it and the video cable makes it look very authentic. These things have worked out very well. Thus far, none of my properties with the cameras have even had an attempted break in.

Wali Dome cameras are less intimidating looking and easier to break.

The only drawback I've ever had from using them was, of course, the tenants. Every single one of them on move in day has asked me, "Do the cameras work?" After informing them that the cameras are dummy cameras, they just don't seem to get it. "How do I get them to come on and do I get a monitor," is usually the next question out of their mouth. It's easier to judge someone by their questions rather than their answers. I'd like to reply, "They're dummies, just like you." I'm sure that they'd get it then. Instead, I have to go into my 5th grade teacher mode and explain to an idiot what a dummy camera is.

Anyway, they're cheap, easy to mount, very effective, and worth every cent!

CHAPTER 15

LANDLORD TIPS

I'm just like a lot of you guys and gals out there because I love to hear a great story too, but when that subject concerns Section 8 rentals and Section 8 tenants, that's even better. My greatest pleasure is coming back in at night, sitting down in front of the computer with a cold glass of Iced Tea, opening up an email from my website, and laughing my ass off! Whether it's a story about a crazy tenant or a tip about a certain product that someone is using to save time or money, I'm all ears.

I swear to you, half of the stories from fellow landlords, I can't even use in the book because the language is beyond rated R. I tell it gritty, a lot of you guys are off the charts! Nonetheless, I sit at my computer and laugh so hard sometimes that I'm afraid that I left my windows open and my neighbors may think I'm a mental patient. So please, please, keep'em coming! Just take a couple of the F bombs out so I can use them.

In the next six chapters, I'm going to get into a couple of the tips that I received from fellow Section 8 landlords that I think were the best to roll in. I'm even considering writing another book just dedicated to landlord tips and stories. I'll call it, "Nightmares of a Section 8 Landlord." Anyway, enjoy the tips.

Wireless Burglar Alarm

Since I was just on the subject of protecting your vacant property, I think that this would be a great time to open up the landlord tip segment from a fellow landlord from Tampa, Florida. This tip comes from Lenny Bowker.

Hello Mike, I enjoyed your books from cover to cover. I don't know if you have used the Honeywell Wireless Burglar Alarm system yet but they are wonderful. What it does is let you alarm your property while you are working on it and as soon as you move your tenant into the property; you simply remove it and use it in your next vacancy. It's basically a temporary alarm system.

I use the Honeywell Lynx Touch 7000L. It costs about $275 and you can get it from their website or on Amazon. It's really slick and very easy to program and set up. It comes with a couple of door and window transmitters which is just enough for me. I don't alarm the upstairs because I don't think that anyone is brazen enough to try to get in with a ladder, but you never know. The company will even send you the sign saying that the house is alarmed to plant in the front yard so that a burglar will know that the house is protected.

I've attached some literature so you can check it out. Thanks for writing the books and keep up the good work!

Thanks Lenny, and yes, I've heard of them but I have yet to use one. I think that they are an excellent idea but thus far, I've had pretty good success with the cheap cameras.

Honeywell wireless burglar alarm.

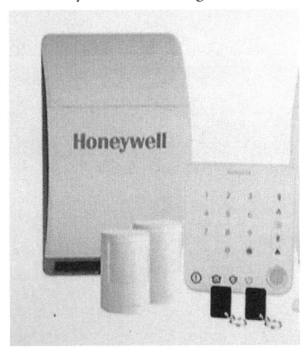

Comes with wireless motion detectors and door and
window transmitters.

CHAPTER 16

DOOR STOP ALARM

Hey Mike, my name is Dawn Gould from Pittsburgh, PA. My husband and I have been in the Section 8 housing business for nearly eight years now and we are up to 40 properties. Not bad for a nurse and a machinist. We were given your books and lease as a Christmas present by my brother in law. At the time, we only had two homes. Your books really motivated us and we went on a tear. Now, we officially have the Section 8 fever!

I'd like to pass on a story and a tip that hopefully you can share with your readers. We purchased a 3 bedroom home on a pretty bad block. Two nights in a row while we were rehabbing the property, crack heads broke into the back door. We had already left the property and locked it down tight for the night, but they still got in. After the first break-in, my husband put screws through the door and into the jam like you showed in your book. The screws that he used weren't long enough and they managed to get in for a second time. That's when I had my Ahha moment.

About a year ago, my husband and I went on vacation to Las Vegas. We purchased a door stop alarm in our hotel lobby for ten bucks. The alarm is to place under your hotel door while you are sleeping so that if anyone such as a maid or housekeeping enters the room, it will alert you. This little thing alerts you in a big way, it's very loud, 120 decibels to be exact and it will pierce your ear drum! Live rock music tops out at 115 decibels so you can imagine how loud this thing is.

What we did was place it under the rear door that they were getting into and hoped for the best. Five days after the last break in, they came back again. The door stop alarm worked like a charm and a neighbor called the police. One guy was apprehended and the other one got away, but they never came back.

I've attached the exact model that we used. You say you're always looking for stories so I thought I'd give you one of ours. Again, loved the books and if you decide to write a Volume 3 and use my story, make sure that I receive the first autographed copy!

Doorstop Alarm

Dawn, I guess what happens in Vegas doesn't always stay in Vegas! Great tip, great story, and yes, I have shipped you out a signed copy of Volume 3. Now, here is my feedback. This is a wonderful solution to a problem area. If someone keeps breaking in through the back door, put the doorstop alarm under the back door and go out the front. Ya see what I'm getting at here, right? You can only use it on one door because you have to go out the other door.

I examined the doorstop alarm and watched several YouTube videos on it. Every property that I own has at least two doors, one in the front, one in the rear, and sometimes a basement door. It is such a great and effective product that it is a shame you can only use it on one door because naturally, you have to leave through the other. 90% of the time that my properties were broken into, it has either been through the front or back door. Rarely do they smash a window because number one, it's very loud, and number two, they don't want to get cut on the glass when entering the property.

Place it under the door and this thing screams if detonated

Dawn, if we could put our heads together and figure out a way to get the alarm under both of the doors and get out of the house without it going off, we could package that sucker up and get it on Shark Tank! By the way, the doorstop alarm that Dawn used was simply called the, "Upgrade Doorstop Alarm." It's the first one that will pop up in Amazon when you search "doorstop alarm." The price varies a little but I have found it for as low as $6.99.

CHAPTER 17

TOILETS THAT SUCK... LITERALLY!

Mike, what's going on brother, it's Joe DiCianni from Queens, New York. I was absolutely blown away by your books; they are so down to earth. I haven't made a move on a Section 8 property yet because every home is pretty expensive up here and the taxes will kill you. I'm down in Philly about four times a year. Maybe next time I'm down I'll hit you up, buy you lunch, and have you run me around through some of your Southwest Philly rentals. If I make a move, it's going to be in Philadelphia.

I've got a great tip for you and I hope you're able to get some material out of it. I own an apartment complex with 16 units in it. The most popular service call that I get is for clogged toilets. I rent to a bunch of senior citizens who pay me a good buck so I'm not as hardcore as you are with my tenants and they are not Section 8, so I do handle the clogged toilet calls.

I finally got smart and started replacing all of their toilets with the High Flow Toilets. I'm sure you've seen or heard of them. They are the ones with the commercials that show them sucking down a dozen golf balls and never clog. Well these toilets are no joke. Since replacing all of the toilets in my complex, I have not had one clogged toilet in nine months. They are very efficient.

They cost a little more but you get what you pay for. I use the American Standard Champion 4, high efficiency 1.6 gallon toilet. I purchased it at Home Depot for $150. Hands down, it is the best $150 that I ever spent.

American Standard Champion 4 toilet

Joe thanks for the email but I already beat you to the punch on this one. I've been using that exact same toilet for about eight years now, I'm the grand wizard. I didn't go door to door ripping all the toilets out of my homes but once I purchase a new home or one becomes vacant, that is exactly what I install. I even put 3 of them in my own home and I'm very happy with them.

I can pick up a regular toilet for less than a hundred bucks but all it takes is one clog that can't be cleared with a plunger, for my tenant to call. Naturally, I tell them when they take possession of the property that the toilet's best friend is the plunger so make sure you own one. Sometimes however, they load it up with 50 feet of toilet paper and now, **you** have a problem if they can't get it cleared and they call the inspector on you.

Also, the water that overflows is going to take out your living room ceiling, carpets, and maybe even the hardwoods under the carpets. Invest the extra $50 bucks that you would pay for a regular toilet and prevent it from happening in the first place. These toilets really work, great tip! The lunch thing I may take you up on, but taking you on a tour of my properties I'll have to pass on. I'm busier than a one legged guy in an ass kicking contest down here.

CHAPTER 18

TUB SURROUNDS

Hi Mike, hope all is well. My name is Javier Ramos and I'm from close to your neck of the woods, Scranton, PA. I purchased your books years ago when I only owned three homes and now I'm up to about thirty. I implemented a lot of your tips over the years but I just had a quick question for you. Have you ever used an outfit called Bath Fitters? You've probably heard of them and know what they do but I used them twice and I was not happy with them. The first time they did a good job but they lied to me on the price. When the sales rep quoted the job, he told me it would be $3,500 but when I got the bill, it was $4,700. I argued with him and managed to get it down a little bit but I still felt ripped off. He told me that once he started the job, there were things that he hadn't previously seen that he had to "customize" so the mold would fit over my existing tub.

I swore that I would not use them again but I got a great deal on a home that needed a new bathtub so I called them back. I was in a pinch and I'm not handy so I really had no other choice. This time I used a different Bath Fitters branch but ended up with shabby work and again, a different price that was quoted to me. At least the first guy did good work! I will never use them again. I was wondering if you have an alternative company rather that Bath Fitters that you may be able to recommend. If so, could you pass their name and number on to me? Thanks in advance and I absolutely loved your books and your writing style is one of a kind. (I seriously don't put these shameless plugs in these stories, but I sure as hell enjoy them!)

Javier, glad you enjoyed the books. Since you're so close to me, next time you need a new tub installed, call me, I'll only charge you $4,600. I'm just kidding. I wish you would have sent me an email before you got into bed with Bath Fitters . . . twice! I would have steered your ship directly away from those pirates. Just take a look at them on "Rip-Off" report or "Scam Alert" on the internet, they're the absolute worse. They feast off of old people and schmucks which makes them worse than pond scum. Look, you sent me a nice email and you purchased my books so I'm not going to call you a schmuck, unless you go for the hat trick and use them again.

Twenty something years ago before the internet was even around, I saw their commercial myself and gave them a call. We had several projects going on and I didn't want to tie my plumber up by having to rip out an entire bathroom, so I'd figured I'd try my luck and get an estimate from them. All I wanted to do was go over the tub and tub walls with that shell that they use so I figured it wouldn't be to expensive and I'd be able to keep my plumber moving along on the other three projects of mine that he was working on. Their concept seemed good and after watching their commercial, it didn't look like an expensive procedure. In fact, I thought I'd save a buck or two but that wasn't the case.

When the sales rep got there, he looked he stepped straight off the used car lot, big goofy glasses, Sears Sucker suit, and a handshake grip that nearly broke my hand. Right after the death grip, he went right into the bullshit. He told me how wonderful the company was, how inexpensive they were, how fast they were with a no mess installation. And then, the boiler room sales technique kicked in! "I'm going to give you a price today but it's only a one day price. If you don't commit today, I'm not going to be able to give you this price ever again. In fact I'll do you a favor kid, and I usually don't do this but you seem like a nice kid. Today and only today I'll knock an extra 10% off, but you have to sign today.

Wow, thanks Jerk-off, now how about spitting the price out, is what I'm thinking. I kept waiting to ask him the price but he kept yapping. It reminded me of an old Foghorn Leghorn line, "I say, I say, the boy talks so much his tongue gets sunburn." Ha, ha, loved Foghorn Leghorn, now back to the story.

Finally he musters up enough nuts to spit the price out, how about $3,200 bucks, and that was 25 years ago! God knows what the price would be today. Now I know why Bath Fitters offers to install a seat in your shower, so you can sit down on it when they give you the bill in case you pass out. I looked him in the face and asked, "Are you out of your F-in' mind?" I swear to you, with a straight face he answers, "We can finance." Yeah, 22% interest ought to take the sting right out of that price. I told him "No thanks" and as I was ushering him to the door, I figured I'd screw with him a little bit. I said, "You look familiar, aren't you that guy who knocked on my door last month trying to sell me that $4,000 vacuum?" Ah, the life of a salesman.

What I'm going to do for you Javier is give you three choices, all of which are much cheaper than Bath Ripper's, I mean Bath Fitters. First, if your tub is in fairly good shape but your shower enclosure walls are in poor condition (this is usually the scenario that I run into 9 out of 10 times), simply leave the tub in tact and go over the shower walls with a tub surround kit, they sell them at Home Depot. I don't care if you're handy or not, watch a YouTube video and you'll have it up in two hours, it's like putting a 3 piece puzzle together. Once it's up, simply caulk where the tub surround meets the tub and you're finished.

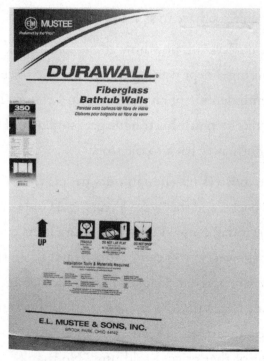

3 piece Durawall tub surround installed

Loctite Power Grab Glue

3 piece Durawall tub surround in box.

The enclosure that we use from Home Depot is the Durawall 3 piece kit. We don't use the real thin, least expensive one and we don't use the decorative expensive one either. The one we use costs $225 bucks, is very thick, easy to install, and holds up very well. After buying the enclosure and tub surround glue, you're in for about $250. That's a total savings of $4,450 compared to your Bath Fitters price. Also, make sure you use tub surround glue and **not** liquid nails. I like to use the Loctite Power Grab glue which goes for about $5 bucks a tube. When you're using the white tub surrounds, you'll be able to see the liquid nails glue lines through the tub surround.

Second choice. Let's say your tub is disgusting to look at. All the paint has faded and is either chipping or peeling away. The tub looks disgusting and filthy but still works perfectly fine. Also, your shower walls are in need of repair.

Solution – Simply have the tub *re-glazed* and again, install the Durawall 3 piece tub surround. To have a tub re-glazed will run you anywhere from $250 to $300 bucks and the tub will come out looking brand new. I know to purchase a new tub may only cost you $150 but don't forget, you have to rip the entire old tub out, pay a plumber to reset a new one, hook up the drain lines, and probably purchase and install a new diverter. Most of the time just re-glazing the tub will save you a lot of time and money. Between the re-glazing and the new tub surround, you're going to put out around a total of $550 bucks. That's still a savings of $4,150 over your Bath Fitters bill.

Before and after of re-glazed tub do to peeling enamel.

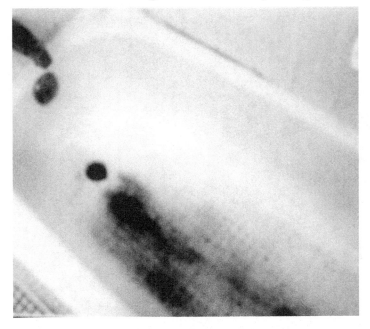

Picture 59 – Caption – Faded tub before glazing.

Picture 60 – Caption – Faded tub after glazing.

Damaged enamel before and after glazing

Third choice – The tub is not salvageable, it's rusted out or has a hole in it and needs to be replaced. Also, the shower walls need to be replaced.

Solution – Rip it out! That's correct, yank the old tub and walls out. Home Depot sells a tub with a 3 piece tub surround kit called the Aquatic. It is very sturdy and it only costs $450 bucks. You are also going to have to purchase a single handle Moen tub and shower diverter. The one that I use is called the Moen Banbury and costs $90 bucks. I'll throw in $600 for labor to install the tub and tub surround so now let's see what we come up with.

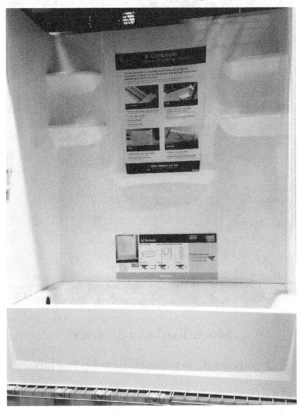

Aquatic tub and tub surround kit

New Aquatic tub and tub surround walls	$450
New Moen diverter	$90
Misc. Parts and Adaptors	$100
Labor	$600
Total	$1,240

Bath Fitters price of $4,700 minus $1,240 = a total savings of $3,460.

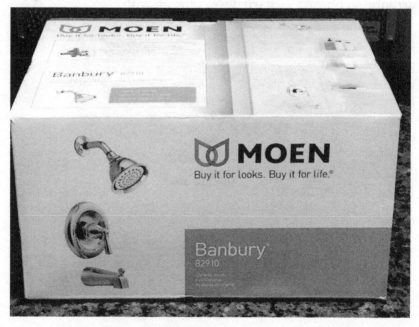

Moen Banbury diverter

Of course if you can do it yourself or shop the labor around for a lower price, you're going to save even more. Remember this, do not overpay for the labor! It's a one day job for two guys and ripping the old tub out and carrying the new one up the steps is the hardest part.

Setting it and tying it in is a breeze, especially if you do it for a living. I pay my guy $400 to set a tub and install a new tub surround but I overestimated the cost for you just to show you that even with the $600 in labor, you're still way ahead of the game over Bath Fitters!

Aloha steel tub $135, great price!

One last scenario that you may come across is if you get a hole in a cast iron tub or if the tub rots out around the drain like they sometimes do when the get very old. If you just have to change the tub, Home Depot sells a cheap 60 inch enameled steel tub called the Aloha for

$135 bucks. I have used them on more than one occasion. They are much lighter than the old steel tubs but they hold up very well and I have no complaints with them and the price is fantastic.

Aloha steel tub $185, great price.

CHAPTER 19

FREE TVS

Hey Mike, I just got done reading both of your books cover to cover. I have never finished reading an entire book in my life, but I breezed through both of yours. Not only were they helpful but my wife and I almost died laughing at some of the shit you guy's talk about and come up with. I can identify with more than half of it because the same stuff has happened to us in one form or another.

I'll pass you on a tip that we have used over the years and it works out nice for us. We are located in Detroit and there are a ton of Section 8 rentals available in the area that we buy in. Sometimes it's hard getting a place rented because people will look at your home and then tell you that they are scheduled to look at five more that day. Of course, they want to pick the nicest one so my wife and I figured out an angle, give them something free!

We decided on a 55 inch RCA that only costs $375. We tell the prospective tenant that if they take the place and we fill out their voucher today, we will give the TV to them as a move in gift and hang it for them on the day they move in. Most of the time they say that they still want to check out other places but then we throw it right back at them and play the same game. We tell them that there are four more showings, which is usually true, set up for today and the first one who takes the house, gets the TV Now, they have a choice to make. Do they risk walking out the door to view a home that may not even be as nice as ours and lose a 55-inch TV or do they sign on the dotted line and get the TV? I'd say it has worked over half of the time for us so we are going to keep doing it.

I know that you're not a big advocate of spending unnecessary money, but I'm not a fan of going back and forth twenty times and showing my rentals. I live almost an hour away from the area that I invest in and it really becomes a hassle. Just thought I'd share!

Leonard Vance

Detroit, MI

Leonard, glad you enjoyed the books and I'm also glad you decided to share your tip! I don't think the money that you spend on televisions equates to, "unnecessary money" at all. Spending unnecessary money would be going over to my tenant's house to paint her kitchen; you're not getting anything out of it. The television tip excels the renting of the unit and that's perfectly fine. The quicker you get the property on the payroll, the quicker your cash is flowing and that is what it's all about. Plus the faster you get it rented; it lessens the chance of having the property broken into while it's vacant. You're giving a potential renter one more reason to pick your house over your competitors, and the TV may just be enough to get it done.

The television may cost you $375 but if you get the home rented two weeks sooner by giving up a TV, you're probably going to break even or be a little ahead of the game. In fact, if I find myself in a bind and can't get one of my properties rented fast enough, I'll incorporate and use this tip myself! Just one question, do they still make 13 inch black and whites? Just kidding, great tip and I won't hesitate to give it a try.

55-inch move-in gift.

Mike's 13-inch move-in gift.

CHAPTER 20

GET ALL OF THE SECURITY MONEY *BEFORE* MOVE IN

Hey Mike, my name is Ian O'Donnell and I'm from Boca Raton, Fl. I also exclusively rent to Section 8 tenants and I have about 40 properties throughout the sunshine state. I enjoyed your books very much and I have a question for you. Have you ever been stiffed by a tenant on the security money? It has happened to me a least five or six times where the tenant falls a couple hundred dollars short of what she needs to bring me on her moving in date and I give in and hand her the keys anyhow. After that, I end up chasing the security money until the day she moves out. Let me know your thoughts on this matter and let me know how you would handle it or prevent it.

Thanks,

Ian O'Donnell

Ian, you're tossing me softballs here! The answer is easy, make sure that you get every dollar off of the tenant before he or she gets the keys to your property. But should you worry about it so much? I know that when I'm meeting a girl at the Section 8 office to sign the lease and I'm expecting her to hand me over two grand but she only pulls $1,600 out of her purse, I'm still signing the lease and grabbing that money. I'll remind her throughout the inspection and the process of waiting for the lease to get drawn up that I will need the full $2,000 on the day that we are to sign the lease, but if she falls a couple hundred short, what am I gonna do?

If I tell her "No deal," the lease doesn't get signed so I'm out $1,100 (first month's rent) right off the bat. I also don't get to grab the $1,600 that's in her hand so now I'm down 2,700 bucks. Plus, now I have to wait for her to come up with the $400 bucks which could take days or weeks, who the F knows? Also, the house now sits there vacant like a target at a shooting range.

You have to pick your battles in this field just like you have to in any other field. Walking away from money and leaving my property vacant is not a battle that I'm ever going to lose. I'm taking the money every time! Look, I'm paying 25k for most of these properties so when someone is waving 10% of my total investment in front of my face, how the hell am I supposed to turn that down? I will draw up a paper while I'm at the Section 8 office saying the woman will pay me $50 per month or whatever, until her security is paid in full, but I rarely get it once they're in the door. If she pays great, if she doesn't, even better! I'll be the one that makes out in the long run.

What do I mean? I'll tell you the truth, I like when they don't pay the security in full. Then they don't expect anything out of me nor are they going to get anything out of me until the security is paid in full, even after they're paid in full, me doing something is iffy. So let's say the woman short changes me on the security and six weeks later she calls to tell me that a burner on her stove is not working. I'd usually come over and take care of it but now I'll tell her to call a stove repair man to fix it, get a receipt, and I'll take it off of the security that she owes me. If she tells me that she doesn't have any money to fix it, I'll tell her that I don't have any money either because I'm short

$400 on the security so it looks like you'll have to use one of the other three burners on the stove that are working. They'll rue the day that they didn't pay the security deposit in full by the time I'm done with'em, LOL! The best part of when they owe you money is they are usually afraid to call you at all because they're afraid you'll ask for it. If you owe someone money, you're not going to pick up the phone to ask them for a loan, right?

I've kept enough security deposits over the years to make up for shortcomings so I'm not really worried about a couple hundred. You are not going to get rich of off security deposits. You get rich by putting a tenant in your place and hopefully cash flowing for years and years to come. Sweating

$400 bucks so much that it makes you walk away from $2,700 bucks would be like stepping over dollars to pick up nickels and although I'm hard headed, I'm sure as hell not foolish.

CHAPTER 21

ELIMINATION

In both Volume I and Volume II, I talked about elimination a lot, I mean a real lot. In fact, it was the tip of the spear. The first two books are about ten years old now and I still remove everything from my rentals now as I was doing twelve years ago, nothing has changed. If I can pat myself on the back for a second here, I'd say that I've done such a thorough job in preparing you to eliminate problems before they ever happen, that I've nearly run out of things to eliminate, and that's a good thing!

What that means is my phone rarely rings for an item in the tenant's home that needs to be repaired. What that means is that rarely does an inspector find an item in my home to fail me on during the inspection. What that means is that if you read the first two books and eliminated all of the items that I spoke of, your inspections should be getting easier and easier to pass. In fact, they should be a piece of cake.

You all know by now that I love the subject of elimination and how important it is so I don't think that I have to drill it into your head that much anymore, I know you get it. Let me just say one more thing about elimination before I get to a couple more items that we found to eliminate and then I'll shut up, I promise. The best way that I can explain why I love to eliminate things is this, "It wasn't raining when Noah built his ark." He could see trouble coming from miles away and he was prepared when trouble showed its face. By planning ahead and removing items that are eventually only going to bite you in the ass down the road, you will be just as prepared as Noah was. Actions speak louder than words but not nearly as often so take action and eliminate problems ahead of time. Now, let's discuss a few things that we found to get rid of and take care of them immediately.

Microwave Ovens

A lot of times, I will purchase a home that has a microwave oven installed above the stove. Years ago, if the microwave worked, I would leave it alone and let the tenants use it. Now when we take possession of a property that has a microwave, I eliminate it. Here's why.

First, the heat coming up from your stove pilots is too much. Between the grease being splashed up and the heat rising up, the microwaves always, and I mean always, quit working. The life expectancy on these things is only about three years, in a rental that is. If your tenant would clean the grease from the microwave, maybe it would last longer but they don't. Now when the thing quits on you, you have a tenant calling you and saying that they want and need a new microwave.

Eliminate the microwave

Second, there is a glass plate that spins around in the microwave. I'd say 90% of the time that a tenant moved out of one of my properties, that glass plate would go mysteriously missing. You can bet that it ended up broken at some time or another. Now when your new tenant takes possession of the property, they will call you and ask you where the glass plate is.

Glass plate will be broken or lost

Third, and this is a 100 percent guarantee, when your tenant moves out, the microwave that you are getting back will be greasy and filthy. The tenant may take the time to clean inside the microwave, but never under it and that is where all the thick grease is. Also, they will never clean the filters which smother the motor and make the microwave burn out. They want their security money back but they won't clean the bottom of the microwave or inside a stove, simply amazing. They will always tell you that they "forgot" to clean the stove and the bottom of the microwave but I think it's more like they don't want to clean them. Guess what? I don't either! I haven't figured out a way to eliminate the stove yet but I'm working on it. So for now, eliminate those microwaves before any of these three scenarios get you!

Filters never get cleaned

In Volume 2, a fellow landlord named Jim Blanch dropped me an email and told me that he uses a stove tin above his stove and I think that was a great idea. It's cheaper than a microwave or an exhaust fan and it will never need a new motor or a light bulb.

A stove tin to prevent a fire is all you need above the stove.

CHAPTER 22

SATELLITE TELEVISION

The next time that you're in the hood, take a look up. What you will see is that nearly every house has some form of a satellite dish bolted to the front of the home, most of the time it's more than one! When your tenant gets satellite TV you get screwed, literally. Here's why.

I count 8 dishes in this picture

First of all, I don't care what company your tenant calls to install their satellite TV, all of their contractors are hacks. Dish Network, DirecTV, Glory Star, Sky Angel, all hacks! Your tenant getting satellite TV should **not** result in you or your property getting destroyed one bit, but it always does. Let's start with the contractors.

6 dishes in this pic- ture

They will take a giant satellite dish and look for a place to mount it on your property. To mount a giant dish, you need a giant bolt. A giant bolt will need a giant hole, four of them in fact. So now this idiot contractor pulls out his hammer drill with the jumbo bit and drives four large holes into your property. Not into the mortar joints, no, no, no, that would be too easy. Instead, he drives the holes directly into your bricks. If he would've put the bolts into the mortar, once the dish was removed, you could simply re-point the joints. Holes in the bricks, they're un-repairable. But wait there's more!

Seriously? The contractor couldn't have used the joints instead of the bricks?

Now that he has the dish securely mounted into your bricks, he now needs a nice size hole to feed the wires through the wall. If you're lucky, he'll use that same hammer drill and pop one more hole in the wall (what's another hole gonna hurt?) Most of the time, you won't be so lucky and he will use a chipping gun and bust a rather large hole through the brick wall so that he has plenty of room to maneuver his wires. Now you're really screwed—but wait there's still more!

With a closer look at the contractor's handy work.

What a great place to smash a hole. Not only can he get the wires through now, but also water, cold air, and mice can find their way in the house.

How to ruin a perfectly good window

Sometimes the idiot will need to splice off and run a separate wire to feed either the upstairs or downstairs. Rather than drilling or smashing another hole through your bricks, he may cut you a break and drill a ½ inch hole through the corner of your brand new vinyl window to feed the cable wire through. What the hell, vinyl is softer than brick so why shouldn't he destroy that too while he's at it. How do I know this? Because it happened to me, four F-in'g times! My brand new $150 windows with a dime size hole drilled in them so my tenant can enjoy the comfort of Dish Network, ain't that nice? Don't try calling and trying to get your money back for the window either because you're just wasting your time. I'm the king of bitching and complaining when I get screwed over and it took me two hours just to get past the operator, after that I was put on the line with Bugs Bunny.

The third thing that they might do to you is mount the dish on your roof. Again, four holes will be drilled directly into your rubber, tar, or shingled roof. Water has a tendency to find its way into any hole sooner than later and you can bet your left ass cheek that it found it's way into one of my rentals. You can bet your right ass cheek that the tenant was the first one to call me and inform me that she has a leak. It was now **war** on satellite television companies and tenants who wanted it installed!

Satellite dish mounted to roof

I couldn't do anything about the tenants who already had it, but I made all of my new tenants taking possession of my properties, sign an addendum agreeing that **no** satellite television is permitted on my property and no dish will ever be installed on any of the walls or roof of the premise. If a dish is ever spotted on my property, it will be grounds for eviction. Also, when a tenant moved out of one of my homes, I had the dish removed and the holes plugged.

Here's 3 mounted to a porch roof

Hey, I get it, times are hard and a lot of my tenants have burned down the bridge with the normal cable companies like Comcast and Verizon by not paying their outstanding bills. However, this does not give you as a tenant, the authority to let a bunch of nitwits make Swiss cheese out of my property by drilling holes all over the place so you can enjoy TV If they owned the house and that's the type of cable that they choose, that's great, but these lazy contractors have destroyed enough of my windows, roofs, and bricks and I've had it. The tenants can either cough up the money that they owe one of these companies, find another outfit that doesn't bolt a dish on my house, listen to the radio, or find somewhere else to live!

CHAPTER 23

HEATERS, A THING OF THE PAST IN MY BOOK

Mike, have you completely lost your mind and started eliminating the heater? Well yeah, sort of. Let me tell you the how and why. We'll start with the "why." Back in the 1990s when we first started out on this journey, government was normal. What I mean by that is that if you, the tenant of a property, used a utility like the water, electric, or gas in the home that you were renting, you were held accountable for the bill. Fair enough right, you use it, you pay for it. How much easier can it get than that?

Well, then big brother stepped in. The utility companies, who I think are the biggest monopolies in the country, decided that they were no longer going to get beat on delinquent utility bills anymore. They lobbied to certain municipalities, such as Philadelphia, came up with a solution, took it to court and won. What was their solution you ask? To hold the **landlords** responsible for the tenant's delinquent utility bills! How fair is that?

The utility companies, who have all the money in the world, hired a pack of corporate dream team lawyers to go into court and get a ridiculous law like this passed. My question was," who was there to represent or fight for the landlord's rights when this law was passed"? Uh, the answer would be nobody. We are not a union, not a monopoly, just a bunch of independent, sole proprietors who the utility companies laid eyes on and said, "These landlords must have deeper pockets than the tenants so let's go after them."

What happens is, let's say your tenant runs up a $500 water bill and moves out of your property. Now you are stuck with their water bill. Totally unfair, you didn't drink one drop of water from their faucet, but you will be paying the bill. Like me, you can cry, scream and stomp your feet, but it won't change a damn thing. You can even refuse to pay it but in the end, they're still going to get you and I'll tell you how. They make the water lien*able,* which means when you go to sell the property the water company is going to be the first one with their hand out to intercept $500 of your money. The lien must be satisfied before the property is sold, total bullshit.

The first utility that was lienable in Philly was the water. I talked about this at great length in Volume I and that is why we started removing hose bibs and washer hook ups. I must say that in the beginning, the water company was pretty fair. If a tenant was 60 days late on her water bill, the water department would come out and turn the water off before the bill got too high. Now, they don't give a shit. They don't really care if the bill becomes four or five months past due before they shut off the water. Why? Because they're gonna get they're money in the end no matter what so what's the hurry? If the tenant pays it and catches up, great, if not, they'll get it out of the landlord's ass. Nick and I wrote a great chapter in Volume 1 on what we do to not get beat on the water bills so I won't refresh it here. I'm just building up to my climax on how and why we eliminated the very costly chore of paying $4,000 bucks to have a heater installed, bear with me.

Okay, so now you have the lawyers from the water company jumping up and down and high fiving each other because they are never going to lose a nickel to a delinquent water bill ever again. Now the gas company looks over their shoulder and sees what the water company pulled off, so now they too decide to get in on the act, they are the next batter up in the order. They hired a pack of corporate lawyers, went into the same courtroom, and came out with the same result, a foot up the landlord's ass! Now gas is also lienable in city of brotherly love.

The gas company works it a little bit differently however. You might say a little fairer but even that's a joke. You shouldn't have to pay one cent for something that someone else used but what are you gonna do? What the gas company has you do is enter into a "Landlord Cooperation Program," which simply means that you are now responsible to police **their** gas or **you** will pay for it. Here are some of the rules on the sign-up form.

1. Registered owner must ensure that Gas Company has prompt and timely access to indoor meters. When requested via email by Gas Company, participant must provide access for any and all shut offs and turn-on of gas.

2. If participant fails to respond to Gas Company within ten days, the participant will be removed from the agreement and held responsible for the gas bill.

3. Participant will be held responsible to keep any and all appointments with Gas Company. Any missed appointments will be considered lack of cooperation and participant will be held responsible for gas bill.

4. The determination whether an owner has provided full cooperation and provided timely access to a meter shall be made solely by the Gas Company.

Like I said, they want you to be the Gas Sheriff. If you want to be protected from gas liens in Philly, before you rent out a property, you have to register into this agreement. You have to give them your phone number and email address and at any moment they can call and harass you to meet the Gas Company at one of your properties so you can give them access to enter and turn the gas off. Do you know how much fun it is to call up a tenant and tell them that you are on your way over to their house to let the Gas Man in to shut off their heat in the dead of winter? The Gas Man becomes enemy number one and you instantly become enemy number two. You see it all the time on the news that a sheriff is killed while serving an eviction and I guarantee you that sooner or later, a utility man and the landlord will be shot while turning off a tenants gas or water, mark my words.

Gas shut off directly out front, why do they need me?

I'm sick that I have to waste my time responding to the gas companies emails, notify my tenants that I'm coming over with the gas company, drive to the property and sit there and wait. When I say wait, it's all the time. They don't say that they'll be there at 10 a.m. No, they give you a window say between 9 a.m. and 2 p.m. And guess what? Half of the time they are the ones that don't show up! Now you break out into panic mode and start calling them so you don't get a lien pinned on you. It's total bullshit. I don't make a nickel off of the gas yet I have to waste my time helping them chase down a dead beat customer. Here is the kicker, there is a gas shut off right out front. All they have to do is bring their gas shut off bar, stick it down the hole, and turn the gas off. What the hell do they have to get into the property for in the first place? Anyway, it's a pain in the ass and like all pains in the ass, I figured out a way to beat'em!

I've talked about both the gas and the water being lienable in Philadelphia. Well the one utility company who hasn't made their service lienable yet is the electric company. That's right, electric is not lienable in Philadelphia, so we took advantage of it! Most of the homes that I purchase have a 40 year old gas heater or oil burner in them that is either on its last leg or needs a complete overhaul. Back in the glory days when gas was not lienable, I would do what I had to do to get the heater up and running or I'd spend several thousand to put in a new heater if it were beyond repair. Oil heaters I didn't even mess around with. I ripped them out and replaced them with gas right away. Not anymore!

Now I use electric heaters. Electric heat has come a long way and it is not as expensive as it once was. What I've been installing in my units is the Cadet Electric heaters. They work terrific; they're cheap, and safe. Here is what I do. Let's say the property is a 3 bedroom home. I'll put a Cadet Com-Pak Twin 4000 in the living room which runs off of a 220 line and believe me, it will put out more than enough heat for the living room and dining room area. It can heat up to an area of 600 square feet in a hurry. In the kitchen, bath, and all 3 bedrooms, I will install a Cadet Com-Pak 1500 watt which runs off of a 110 line and will heat an area up to 200 square feet. I like to keep each heater on its own separate electric breaker so they won't trip. Each heater has its own individual thermostat.

Cadet Com-Pak's are easy to install and look nice.

The Cadet Com-Pak Twin 4000 costs me $175 and the Cadet Com-Pak 1500's cost me $115 a piece. So for $750 bucks, I'm heating the entire house rather than putting out $4,000 to install a new heater and the best part is that I don't have to put up with the gas companies nonsense. The stove and the water heater are still gas but they don't rack the gas bill up like the heater does and when my tenant gets a low gas bill, nine out of ten times, they pay it. I don't really care if their electric bills increase because of the electric heaters because the electric is not lienable and doesn't affect me in any way, shape or form. I could care less if the electric company has to come out and turn off the electric, they won't need my help in doing it. Also, 90% of Section 8 tenants are on what is called the budget with the electric company which means that no matter what amount that their electric bill is, they may only have to pay thirty or forty bucks.

This tip is also going to come in handy for someone who is purchasing a shell and had $4,000 earmarked for a new heater. Now all you have to do is shell out the $750 for the Cadet heaters and you're in business. Take the extra money and put it into a new kitchen and bathroom. If I only have enough money to rehab the kitchen or the bathroom, I **always** choose the kitchen! The reason for this is simple. It's the first room that a perspective tenant is going to see and it might just persuade them into renting your property. Remember, you want the property to rent as soon as possible and having a new kitchen instead of a new heater is way more visible. A new heater means nothing to a renter because if it quits working, they're simply going to call you anyway.

I've been using these things for several years now and I've had zero problems or complaints. When something works that well for me, I'll stick with it! I even put one in my basement at my home. They are a tad bit louder than when your gas heater is blowing out of the vents but like I said, I haven't had any tenants complain about the noise yet and if they do, I'll pass out earplugs when they sign the lease! You can check out all of their products at cadetheat.com.

CHAPTER 24

ELECTRIC BASEBOARDS

Okay, if you don't like the idea of the Cadet heater, maybe you'll like this one, baseboard electric heaters. This is really for the cities where the gas is lienable. The electric baseboard heat is more expensive than the Cadet heater but serves the same purpose which is, you are now heating the home with electric rather than gas so you do not get stuck with someone else's gas bill. One plus in using the baseboard heaters as opposed to the Cadet heater is they are quieter. The Cadet heater has a blower motor on it that you can hear a little bit but it's nothing to get worked up about.

You can pick the baseboard heaters up rather inexpensive also. I use the Reznor EBHB-15 Heavy Duty Electric Radiator. I pay $140 bucks for a 5 ½ foot length. They weigh about twelve pounds and are very easy to install. Once they are mounted, I have my electrician tie them all in to the same thermostat. I'll use two of them in the living room, two in the dining room, and then one each in the bedrooms, kitchen and bathroom. I've had on an occasion or two, to install two of them in some of my homes with bigger kitchens. So basically in a three bedroom home, I use 9 of them for a total of $1,260 plus tax, wire, and the thermostat and you're looking at about $1,500, which is still way cheaper than installing a gas, forced hot air unit, plus you don't have to worry about any gas bills.

You can check out their product line at reznorhvac.com but listen to me, if you are going to have an electrician put these things in for you, don't get ripped off! $400 bucks is the most that I would ever pay anyone to do this job. It's a one day, very clean and very simple job. Remember, he's tying wires together, not operating on your heart!

General Information

Type	Baseboard
Product Line	EBHB
Medium ⦿	Electric
Model	EBHB-8-AK3E

Performance

Heating Capacity	2561 BTU
Nominal Heating Capacity	3000 BTU

Electrical Data

Voltage	240 Volts
Phase	1
Frequency	60 Hz

Dimensions

Product Height	5.1875 Inches
Product Width	37.1875 Inches
Product Depth	2.4375 Inches
Product Weight	7 Pounds

Warranty Information

Parts Warranty	1 Year
Heat Exchanger Warranty	Lifetime Years

Certifications

Country of Origin	United States
CSA Listed	Yes

Reznor General Information

CHAPTER 25

AVOID CRAIGSLIST

One of the most important subjects that I touch on in my books is "street smarts." Either you have them or you don't. If you don't, you can learn them very easy with these two tips, speak to no one and trust no one! Or you can learn street smarts the hard way. If you purchase a property and you see drug dealers on the corner, walk down there and tell them that you've purchased a home on the block and you're not going to tolerate this type of behavior. When they split your head open and take your wallet, you've just learned the hard way. 90% of trouble often begins when we involve ourselves in other people's business, the other 10% of trouble you can learn to avoid.

Being a Section 8 landlord is as safe or as dangerous as you make it. Nick and I have been in a million verbal arguments with our tenants. We've been threatened and challenged to fights on a couple of occasions also. Never have either one of us jumped in our trucks and went over to our tenant's house to answer the bell, which would be stupid and looking for trouble. I don't have to prove my manhood to some of these morons. You can be the toughest guy in the world but you can't beat up a bullet.

Both of us have gone at it nose to nose with a couple of tenants also, sometimes you can't avoid it. I guess I'm very lucky with my big mouth that none of these arguments have ever spilled out into the street. When you're dealing with your tenants, believe it or not, you're safer than you are when you are dealing with strangers. You know who your tenants are and they know who you are so if anything goes down, there will be consequences to pay. They may lose their voucher and you may lose your right to participate in the Section 8 program, so we've both got a line in the sand that we can't cross. I know of two Section 8 landlords who have crossed this line by going to blows with their tenants. One guy had 88 properties and Section 8 barred him from the system because he broke his tenant's 19-year-old son's cheekbone. He was forced to evict all 88 tenants because Section 8 was no longer paying him for any of his properties. He was considered a risk and they dropped him faster than a hotel maid drops a used rubber when she picks it up off your dresser.

It's the people that you come across that you don't know that present the most danger. They don't know you from a can of paint and you don't know them so they already think that they have the edge. If they try to rob or assault you, you can't just tell the police their name and where they live like you could a tenant so the police would have to physically apprehend them and that's not always an easy task in the city. One place where you will come into contact with a lot of these strangers is if you use the Craigslist Site to rent your property.

Craigslist can be a dangerous place to list your property

Since the site was created, about a million bad things have happened to people using Craigslist! Whether someone shows up to purchase a car and gets bonked over the head and their money stolen or a woman shows up for a blind date and gets raped or murdered, you name it and it has happened to someone using this site. For someone who is not street smart, Craigslist is bad news! Renting houses through this website is no different.

First let me start by saying that I have used this site many times and I have had no problems, but I don't rent my houses from it. I have purchased a cement mixer, a bobcat, a boat, and several other things on there and the deals always went smoothly. Two landlords that I know personally weren't so lucky.

The first guy got ripped off . . . twice! The first time someone called him to set up a showing on one of the properties that he had listed on the site. When he pulled up to the property, a guy and what appeared to be a girl with a Muslim head scarf covering her head were waiting on the front steps. He opened the door to the property and as quick as he stepped inside, they had the door closed and a gun under his chin. The person wearing the Muslim gear turned out to be a guy and demanded the guy's wallet, watch, phone, and of course they drove off with his brand new 2014 Ford F-250. Think he learned his lesson? Nope!

He was smart enough to realize that when he was robbed, the incoming number that the thugs called him from was restricted. Either the thugs dialed *67 before dialing his phone number to make the call come up restricted or they actually called from a restricted number, but whatever the case may be, the landlord didn't take any more calls from restricted numbers. Think that will stop a thief? No way! The next time that he got ripped off, he had an actual phone number come up on his phone, so he thought he was safe. Also, he went out and got his gun permit after I convinced him to. He kept telling me that he'd probably never need a gun again. I told him that I'd rather have a gun and not one instead of needing a gun and not have one. Once you hit 40 years old, you're too young to die and you're either too old or too fat to run so make sure you protect yourself.

Anyway, he gets a call from Craigslist from a guy that wants to see the property. He feels a lot safer now and meets the guy at the property, lets him in and lets him look around. He told me he didn't want the guy to feel like he was up his ass so he let the guy mosey around the house while he waited at the front door for him to finish his tour. That's something that I never do! The guy tells him that he wasn't interested in renting the property and he leaves, as does the landlord. What the landlord did not know is that the perspective renter unlocked the basement door. He came back later that night and ripped out all of the copper and even took the brand new stove. (Get yourself into the habit of checking to see if all the doors and windows are locked after each time you show your rental. It's easier to prevent bad habits than it is to break them).

The phone that the copper thief called from was traced back to one of those Boost phones where you just pay for the minutes and nobody, not even the police know who the hell owns the phone. If he would have just been doing what I have been doing for years, he could have prevented both of these robberies.

1. I only rent to Section 8 tenants and they must have their packets with them before I show them the property. If they don't have the packet, I don't open the door. Like the Asian lady at the Laundromat tells me when I go to pick up my clothes, "No ticky, no shirty."

2. I will ask them to see the packet before I even open the door. I want to know who I am showing the property to. Second, I want to view if their voucher is a 2 or 3 bed- room voucher which will be clearly stamped on her paperwork. I'm not opening the door and wasting my time or energy showing a woman with a 2 bedroom voucher a 3 bedroom home. If the name on the packet matches the name that the woman gave me on the phone and the bedroom numbers match, its open sesame, if not, so long.

3. No boyfriends or men are permitted to view the property and if there is going to be any trouble, well, that's why I carry a gun. I won't even bother getting out of the truck if the woman is waiting on the steps with a male. I'll wave her over and tell her to send him on his way. If she doesn't, I go on my way.

4. Never, and I mean **never,** do I let a perspective tenant stroll around my property unat- tended. They are not going to unlock a door or window that they can crawl back in through later and rip me off. Not gonna happen!

5. If they show up with children and we get split up along the tour, when the showing is over I will walk back around the property and make sure that all the doors and windows are locked before I leave. I'm the tour guide so I'm the guy unlocking and locking back up all the doors. You can't trust anyone these days.

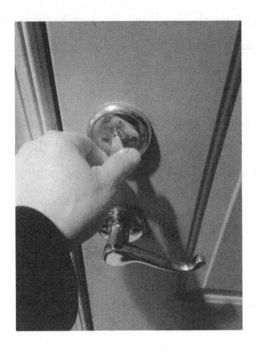

Always make sure the doors and windows are locked after showings

The Second Landlord who used Craigslist and Lost

Okay, after talking to this guy, this is an assumption, but a pretty good assumption that I think I'm 99% right on. Here is what happened. The landlord ran an ad on Craigslist for a "property for rent." A guy calls him and sets up a showing. He and the landlord meet at the property. The perspective tenant is a black guy, about 6 ft. 2, skinny, missing a tooth with a beard. The guy asks the landlord if he can take some pictures to show to his wife and he will get back to the landlord after his wife views the pictures, she couldn't be at the showing because she had a broken leg was the story. Anyway, the landlord agrees, and the guy takes a bunch of pictures, but never calls back.

Three days later the landlord has another showing and drives up to his property. Something was not right he instantly realized when he saw curtains hanging in the windows. He walks up to his property and lets himself in. What do you know, there's a guy sleeping on a couch in the home which is now completely furnished, pictures and everything hanging on the walls! The guy on the couch jumps up and asks, "Who the hell are you?" which is exactly what the landlord was wondering.

I'm going to try to make a long story short here. The guy who was sleeping on the couch told the landlord that he rented the place from guess who? You got it, a skinny black guy about 6 ft. 2, missing a tooth with a beard. He said he saw the ad on Craigslist (pictures and everything), gave the guy with the beard $1,800 (first month, last month, and a month security), and signed a lease which he had in his possession. The cops were called out but since the guy had a lease, even though the landlord's name was not on it, there was nothing that they could do. The landlord was told that it was a landlord/tenant dispute and it would have to be settled in court. The landlord went downtown, filed for an eviction and it took him over three months to get the guy out. Meanwhile, the guy runs up a $400 water bill and a $500 gas bill.

The landlord assumes that the bald guy missing a tooth that he showed the property to broke into the property and changed the locks so that he would have a key. That way, a perspective tenant would assume that he was the owner. He then ran an ad on Craigslist himself for a "property for rent." He posted a home, with pictures, that would normally rent for at least $1,000 per month, for $600 per month so that it would rent in two minutes at that low asking price. After that, the landlord assumes the guy rented the home to the unsuspecting guy that was on the couch and laughed all the way to the bank with his $1,800 bucks. This could indeed be the case, but I seriously doubt it.

Here is what I think happened. I think that it was a set-up from the beginning. I think that the bald guy with the beard knew the guy on the couch who moved into the property, they were both in on it. Squatters will pull this kind of bull shit because they know that they can get away with it. Once they are in the property and have some form of story and a bogus lease that you can purchase at Staples for five bucks and fill out, it now becomes, just like everything else, the landlord's job to get them out of the property. How F'ed up is that?

You would think that a tenant would also have to do a little leg work and also be held a little responsible for whom they are renting from and handing over money to, but that's simply not the case. I mean, how hard would it be for the tenant to have to ask the landlord for a photo ID and a copy of his rental license before signing a lease and forking over a couple grand? Just by making the renter ask the landlord for those 2 things and to be held responsible to get a copy of them, it would totally eliminate the "Squatter's Rights" bull shit and the courts would never have to spend another nickel on hearing these cases, but they won't. The politicians passing these laws should be shot. Politicians and diapers should be changed regularly, and for the same reason, they're both full of shit. Not one law favors the landlord and when you get in front of a liberal judge, half the time they want to mount a defense for the tenants! I feel like saying, "Hey pal, your job is not to mount a defense; it's to hear the case and make a decision, that's it. If you want to go back to defending people, go back to being a lawyer." Sorry, I had to vent. Now back to the story.

I did learn one rather important tip from this landlord's story, other than don't use Craigslist. He told me that when the cops pulled up and he told them what was going on, the cops asked him if he had a "No Trespassing" sign in the window.

He answered, "No" and asked them why. The cops told him that if he had proof that a "No Trespassing" sign was posted, they would be able to remove the squatters for trespassing because it was clearly posted and trespassing is **not** a landlord/ tenant dispute. How stupid is that? The laws and the red tape that you have to cut through these days to get anywhere are sickening. Anyway, the moral of the story if you don't want squatters in your property, simply hang a sign in the window.

No trespassing sign can prevent squatters

Here is what I do since hearing this nightmare. The minute that a tenant moves out of one of my properties or I purchase a new one, I place my "No Trespassing" sign in the window, and then I go out front and take a picture of it with my phone so that it's time stamped. I also have Nick video record me hanging the sign in the window. Make sure that you get enough of the house, an address if possible, into the picture so that there will be no doubt that this is the house that you hung the sign in. Then, I **remove** the "No Trespassing" sign! I now have proof that there was a sign hanging in the widow, but I don't need a copper thief seeing the sign and putting two and two together that the home is vacant.

I haven't had a squatter move into any of my properties and I haven't been stuck up in any of my properties. If I keep avoiding Craigslist, there is a pretty good chance that neither one of these things will ever happen to me. In the next chapter, I'll tell you how I get my properties rented, the safe way.

CHAPTER 26

GOSECTION8.COM

First of all, I still list my available units with PHA (Philadelphia Housing Authority). My property, my name, and my phone number are put into a huge list and distributed to Philadelphia section 8 tenants who are searching for a property to rent. I believe the list is renewed every month and this method has worked for me for years. Most of all, I like it because it is free, but I believe I have found something more effective and it gets my vacant homes rented faster! Still, if you are in an area where you can list your property for free on a housing authority website, take advantage of it. Free never hurt anyone.

Over the past couple of years, I have been listing my vacant homes on a website called GoSection8.com and I've had a ton of success renting from this site. GoSection8.com is a website for landlords, tenants, and housing authorities who participate in the Section 8 program.

GoSection8.com works well for renting section 8 units

I have a "premium membership" which costs $33 per month and I'll tell you why it works better than just throwing my property on a list like I do with PHA.

1. Your listings never expire! They never come down until you take them down. You don't have to go through the hassle of relisting and relisting.

2. Top placement! With the premium membership I jump right over everybody who is not a premium membership member. My listings will always appear at the top of the page.

3. Pictures. I can attach a ton of pictures to my ad so the perspective tenant can see exactly what the house looks like. That way, they are not wasting your time with a showing if they're thinking that they are coming to see the Taj Mahal.

4. Phone and email tracking. All calls and emails to your listings are tracked online. They have a tracking interface that lets you see all connected calls, caller ID, and email messages. I find that gives you an edge in safety because you now know who is coming to see the property before they get there because you have a solid phone number and email address.

There are a couple more things that GoSection8.com will do for you if you list your property on their site and I highly recommend them. Other than my website, I know of no other site that caters directly to us Section 8 landlords so give them a play, it works for me!

CHAPTER 27

FINDING GOOD TENANTS

In this chapter, I'm going to talk about one of the things in the industry that have changed over the past couple of years, for the worse! Finding a good tenant to move into one of my properties is becoming a little bit of a hassle.

When we first started out investing in Southwest Philly, I'd say that the neighborhood was about 5% rentals and 95% homeowners. Now you're looking at about 50% renters, 50% homeowners which is not really a great place to find a good tenant. I sugarcoat nothing in my books, never have, and I never will. Once you start getting rental saturation in an area, the crime rate will go up and your quality of tenant will go down. Finding a good tenant gets tougher and tougher because a good tenant usually doesn't want to live in a high crime area.

Notice that I didn't say, "Tougher to rent"? I said finding a good tenant gets tougher, I can always grab a Section 8 tenant and throw her in my property and start collecting $1,100 per month, there's no shortage of tenants. The shortage is on finding the really good tenants that want to make the place a home and respect your property. I told you in Volume I how I would go over to the tenant's home to drop off their completed voucher and do a quick run through of the house that they were living in to see what kind of condition it was in. If it wasn't too bad, I'd rent to them. Well now what I'm finding is more and more homes that I walk through are pretty bad according to my standards. I've been handing more vouchers back to the perspective renters and saying, "No Thanks!" Some landlords would still rent to them but I'm a little weird. A little dirty, yeah, I can handle that because it's not going to fail me on my annual inspection. But when I look around and see things broke, dollar signs go off in my head.

Most of the time when I'm doing my tour of their property, they want to walk beside me and make excuses for everything that is busted up in the house. The number one excuse is that their landlord is a "Slumlord" and he doesn't want to fix anything. They tell me that because the landlord doesn't want to fix things, this is the reason that they are moving, really? What a shame. I can't understand why your landlord wouldn't want to come over here and repair the iron holes that you put in his carpet while ironing on the floor, or why he wouldn't run a 5 gallon bucket of spackle over so he can patch all the holes that someone punched in the walls, or why he doesn't hire a search team to find out where all the stove knobs got to. The beat goes on with them and listen, I'm the number one guy in the world that you shouldn't be telling that your landlord, "doesn't want to fix anything," because I not only don't want to fix shit, I don't even want to hear you call me on the phone!

Ten years ago, I would deny maybe one out of ten people who were trying to rent a home from me and I thought that was bad.

Now I deny about three out of ten and I'm even more lenient now than what I was back then. What the hell is going on! Sometimes I leave their house grossed out and checking my clothes for hitching roaches that also want to get the hell out of there. It's the time that you have to invest in finding a good tenant that's taking longer and longer and that is what the pain in the ass is. Once you deny a tenant, you have to start the entire rigmarole over again and it sucks but I'm not yet ready to gamble on a tenant that promises she won't bust my property up like the one she is currently doing it to now. In my personal life, I like to gamble and I don't skirt it. Nothing to serious, I'll throw $200 bucks on a football game or on a craps table faster than a cat can lick his ass but I'm not yet ready to start gambling with destructive tenants who will destroy my property. Hell, I've got a chance to win when I gamble. Here is where I know that I have a screw loose.

About a month ago my carpet cleaner who charges $150 bucks to steam clean an entire house pulls up and tells me that before he gets started, he wants me to know that his price went up to

$200. I ask him when the hell did this happen because he just did a job for me last week and it was only $150. He informs me that today's the first day of his, "price change." I said, "Wow, how lucky am I? I'm probably your biggest customer and I give you tons of jobs yet I'm the first one to get your increase stuck up my ass. Wind your hose up and put your carpet wand away, I'll find someone else that can do it for $150 or cheaper, with the volume of work that I give you it shouldn't be hard." Of course, he came to his senses and lowered his price back down to $150 bucks but I'm not willing to pay someone $200 bucks for a one-hour job. That's $1,600 a day that he would be earning and that's insane! My point being, I'll argue with anyone at any time to save fifty cents, yet I have no problem putting $200 bucks on a football flying around in the air for three hours. How the hell does that make sense? My priorities are a little whacked out sometimes. Where was I now, oh yeah, I was running out of a disgusting house and checking my clothes for hitching roaches.

I know why it's getting harder to find good tenants and the answer is location. Twenty years ago, the area that I was investing in was a good area, so you got good families that wanted to live in that area. The schools were good and the neighborhood was safe. Now it's a high crime area and if a tenant is willing to move her family into a high crime area, well you're probably not getting real good tenant. I'll give you the "two oceans" analogy. One ocean is full of sharks and parents are letting their children swim there and get eaten alive. The other ocean, which is 20 miles away, is shark free and no one is getting eaten alive. A parent has a choice and if she chooses to bring her children to the ocean full of sharks, then she is not a good parent. The parent, who keeps her kids safe by traveling to the shark free ocean, is a good parent. That was simple enough to understand, right?

The good news is that I'm not looking for a "real good tenant." I'm just looking for a tenant who is not going to destroy my place and pay their portion of the rent if they have one, that's it. I'm easy to get along with and as long as the property passes inspection every year and you don't blow up my phone asking me to repair things that you broke, I won't even bother with you.

There is a solution to this problem but I'm not yet willing to take the leap. The solution if you wanted to find a better quality of tenants would be to buy in better neighborhoods. Renters that look at neighborhoods such as Southwest Philadelphia and say, "Hell no, I'm not letting my family live there," are probably going to make for better tenants but that's no guarantee either. They might expect more and be a bigger pain in the ass. Also, if you're going to venture into better neighborhoods, be prepared to pay more for your property and the real estate taxes will certainly be higher, which will eat into your bottom line. I'm telling you, you can make a fortune in these "not so desirable neighborhoods." You just have to put up with a little more of the bullshit and to me it's worth it!

Where else are you going to pay 25k for a property, yank a 50k mortgage out on it, and stick 25k profit in your pocket before a tenant even walks through the door? Nowhere! Now after your tenant does take possession of the property, it gets even better. Your mortgage including taxes and homeowner's insurance is going to come in at $400 bucks a month and you're renting the property for $1,100 bucks a month. That's a $700 profit for sitting on your ass for thirty days. Most people have to punch a clock for 40 hours to get $700. If you want to think small, that's fine. String ten of these properties together in the fashion that I just talked about and now you're looking at

$7,000 a month for doing nothing but collecting a check. The numbers and the possibilities are endless and if you set your mind to it, there is nothing that you cannot achieve! It may be a "not so desirable" area for some people but for Nick and I it's a goldmine, and it could be for you also, if and when you find that niche neighborhood to start renting in and building your own empire! They're out there.

CHAPTER 28

PRIDE!

This chapter is about pride, something that I don't think I would have ever talked about had it not been for my website and the phone calls that I do. I'd say that about half the people that I talk to during my phone conversations are on the fence about purchasing a property and renting it out to a Section 8 tenant. You would thing that they are on the fence about getting involved because of a lack of money or finances but to my surprise, that is not the case. Most of these people have a mental block to get through first and that mental block is their *pride.*

Pride is not always a good thing, especially when it comes to real estate and I'll tell you why. First, let me start by saying that it's great to take pride in things such as your appearance. You know, put on some nice clothes, work out a little bit, drive a clean car, get a fresh haircut and it shows that you take pride in yourself which is great. Real estate investing is a totally different ballgame. A lot, and I mean a lot of people or I wouldn't be writing about it, can't get past the fact that they are going to be purchasing a property in a lower end area and renting it to Section 8 tenants. They like the numbers but for some reason, they believe that owning this type of property is beneath them. Their pride is getting in the way of their wallets! They want me to talk them into it, which I usually do, but it's the numbers that should be talking them into it, not me.

Here is exactly what most of the on-the-fencer's ask me. "Wouldn't it be better if I go out and purchase a 150-thousand-dollar home and rent it to a middle class family? I can pull a 150k mortgage that would equate to a $1,100 a month payment and then I can rent the property out for $1,100 per month. Even if I don't make a nickel off of the rent, after thirty years the tenant will have paid the house off for me without the hassle of Section 8 inspections and I can now sell the property and stick a 150k profit in my pocket?"

My answer is always; sure, you could do that but let's sharpen our pencils, do a little math, and see who comes out on top. There is no way that you are going to get away with putting $0 into your property over 30 years so your assessment of a "150k profit" on your middle class property is far fetched but just to prove a point, I'll give you a 150k profit just for the hell of it. Now, let's do it my way.

We'll say that I pull a 60 thousand dollar mortgage on a Section 8 rental in a lower class neighborhood. The mortgage payment would be around $550 bucks which includes taxes and insurance. I receive $1,100 per month through the Section 8 program for the rent. That's a profit of $550 per month, a 50% return on your money. Over one year, you will have collected a profit of

$6,600 ($550 x 12 months = $6,600). Over 30 years, you will have collected $198,000 ($6,600 x 30 years = $198,000). Then add the $198,000 to the $60,000 that you can now sell your property for and that gives you a total of $258,000. You're $108,000 ahead of the middle class property purchase and your investment was $90,000 less!

The question I ask them is, "Do you want to get rich and build a solid monthly residual income renting lower end properties or do you want to keep your pride intact and tread water renting middle class properties?" I'll take the money every single time! When I was a kid, I'd hear old timers say, "I'd shovel shit if the price was right." Now I get it. If you could shovel roses for a dollar per shovel full or you could shovel shit for five dollars a shovel full, which one would you choose? If you picked the roses, then you're probably not cut out for the life of being a Section 8 landlord.

Don't ever be embarrassed about what you do for a living and never let your pride stand between you and making a buck. Hell, some of my friends and even my mom joke with me and call me a slumlord. Many of my friends have different types of smarts that lead them to careers in science, chemistry, or teaching, but they don't make as much as me! My smarts ended up being in making money in lower end rentals and I wouldn't change a thing. Call Nick and I bottom feeders or slumlords, call us whatever you want but the facts are, we are really great at making money in these lower end neighborhoods and you can do it too, there is a ton of money to be made in them! Rich as well as poor people are always going to need a place to live and if you end up being their housing provider, you are always going to be in the driver's seat and be able to make a good buck. A lot of people have used Section 8 rentals as a stepping stone to get involved in real estate and once they have put some cash in their pocket, they moved on to bigger and better things, which is also fine. For me, this is my lane and I stay in it. I love the small initial investment with the big monthly return. I always say volume is what makes you rich in this game and with the small 25k to 30k investment on a lower end property; I can get my numbers up in a hurry. Maybe someday, ocean front properties will be what I'm investing in but for right now, I'm happy right where I'm at!

CHAPTER 29

PLAYING DIRTY, THIS TIME WITH LAWYERS

Anyone who has ever read my books knows exactly how I feel about lawyers and judges! Well, you can lump insurance companies in with them also and if I ever hear from the three of them again in my life, it will be too soon. I'm sure there are some good lawyers out there who have really helped some people get well deserved settlements. Let's say you were injured by a drunk driver or lost a love one due to medical malpractice and a lawyer got you a huge settlement, then you deserve it. That's the type of lawyer that I can appreciate. When an honest victim is injured by someone's obvious negligence, then I agree that the victim should be awarded a monetary settlement. That's **not** the ambulance chasers and scammers that I'm dealing with!

I've been sued seven times since I've been in this business and I remember every single lawsuit because they were all bogus! One case had a chance to maybe be legit but I have a problem with that one too. I don't bullshit and if there was one case that I felt was deserving of a nickel, I'd tell you. If someone was electrocuted half to death by faulty wiring in one of my homes or a roof caved in on a family's head, I'd say hey, that's what insurance is for, pay the man. But when I say bogus, I mean bogus. Here are a few examples that some of these numbskulls have brought against me.

A) We had a blind guy living in a two bedroom home. His rent portion was $70 bucks a month and he got two months behind on his rent portion. Since he's blind and lived three doors down from our shop, I went over and knocked on his door so I can hand him his eviction letter and tell him why he's being evicted. Five days later I got a call from his lawyer telling me the guy tripped over shoes that **he** left on the steps and took a spill down the steps. I turned it over to my insurance carrier and they settle with the guy for $4,000. That's correct, I freaking lost to a blind guy that left his own shoes on the steps and tripped over them. How the hell am I supposed to prevent that?

B) A woman who was also in the process of being evicted overflowed her toilet. The water went through the bathroom floor and started pouring into the living room be- low. Instead of plunging the toilet or turning off the main water valve like any other normal human being would do, she decides to go into the living room at exactly the same spot where the water is pouring down and look up. At that exact moment, wouldn't you know it, a wet card- board ceiling tile gave way and came down striking her in the face and of course injured her neck. We're talking about a piece of wet card- board that might weigh two pounds. Again, a lawyer calls and again my asinine insurance company pays, this time $4,800 bucks. A ten year old wouldn't believe this woman's story but the chicken shit insurance company didn't want to take the risk in court, so they paid. Also, it would cost them a couple grand to defend the case so they threw a low offer out and paid the woman just to get rid of the case. Meanwhile the next year, my insurance went up $25 bucks per property. When you have a lot of properties, that increase hurts. Look, I don't care if they pay claims out like their giving out candy, but don't increase my rates if you're not going to fight back, that's what I'm paying for!

This cost me $4,000.

These two lawsuits were filed against me in my early years of being a Section 8 landlord. I've smartened up a little since then and had my tenants start signing a "Can Not Sue" addendum (which is in my lease), before they take possession of the property. What it states basically is that anyone who is on the lease gives up their right to sue the landlord. This addendum alone probably saved my ass a hundred times.

I don't know if you picked up on the common thread of the first two lawsuits that I discussed with you but if you didn't, I'll fill in the blanks. 90% of the lawsuits filed against me were from tenants who were being evicted. In their crazy minds, they figure you're screwing them so they might as well do the same too you, it's kind of like a going away gift from them. They have nothing to lose and everything to gain. Some gold-digging lawyer will take their case no matter how absurd it is. You on the other hand, have a lot to lose! First, you'll see a spike in your insurance rates and second, if enough claims are filed against you, the insurance company has the right to drop you on the spot or not renew your policy when it expires. Whether you're like me and have a good amount of properties or you're just starting out and have three or four properties, once an insurance company drops you it's nothing but a pain in the ass trying to find a new insurance carrier that will insure your rentals.

You'll have to explain why you were dropped and if the carrier that you are trying to insure with sees you as a risk, they can and probably will tell you to knock on someone else's door. When you do finally find someone who does answer the door, best believe you will be quoted a high rate.

The greatest thing about my "Can Not Sue" addendum is that it usually cuts off the head of the snake before it has a chance to bite. From my past experiences, what usually happens when a tenant is getting ready to sue you, they'll call you up and tell you that they had an accident in your home or on your property. Whether they fell down the steps and your railing pulled out of the wall or at the precise moment a globe from the light fixture fell, they were standing right under it and it landed on their head, you'll be the first to get that dreaded bullshit call.

When you tell them to look at their lease and remind them that they signed an addendum that forfeited their right to sue you, they'll bitch and moan and 90% of the time, that's the end of it. As all of my stories go, I wrote these books about the 10% of the time your nightmares come true! In this case your nightmare is a lawyer. Once in a while you'll get that tenant who, even know they signed the addendum, they still want to contact an attorney to see what he or she can do for them.

The attorney will look directly at the addendum, and do you think that they will pass on the case? Does an elephant pass the peanuts? No! The addendum will bluff 90% of the tenant's away but, and I hate to say this, an attorney is smart enough to know that an insurance company will cough up the money to settle small claims all day long. Why? It's simple, because it's cheaper to settle them than it is to fight them. Even know my insurance company's attorney could have walked in the courtroom and handed the judge the "Can Not Sue" addendum and squashed the tenant's case, it would cost them more money to hire an attorney to fight it.

After inserting my addendum into my lease, I was only sued a total of five more times over the last twelve years. With hundreds of properties and only five lawsuits, I guess I'm pretty lucky, had I not inserted the addendum into the lease, I'm quite sure it would have been a lot worse. Most of the lawsuits were settled for peanuts with the biggest award being $7,200 bucks. They are as follows:

1. A twelve-year-old girl was bit by a neighbor's dog on my property. She wasn't my tenant and it wasn't my tenant's dog but since it happed on my property and the guy who owned the dog didn't have homeowner's insurance, my insurance company shelled out $7,000.

2. After a snowstorm, one of my tenants didn't shovel her walkway. She was in the process of being evicted of course. Well the story was that her aunt came over the house, fell on the ice and hurt her back. My insurance company paid the woman $5,500 even know she had eleven similar slip and fall cases.

3. Another slip and fall which is the legit one but I still have a problem with it. A 65-year-old guy tripped over the gas shut off cap which stuck up out of the sidewalk about an inch. He broke his wrist, the gas company paid him $11,000 and my insurance company paid him $5,000. Here is the kicker, the gas cap was on my neighbor's property, but he fell onto mine. Of course, the neighbor didn't have insurance, so they got it out of my insurance company's ass.

4. This one, 100% bogus! A tenant of mine said she had the window open and out of nowhere the window just came slamming down. Where do you think her fingers were at that exact time? You guessed it, directly inside the windowsill. She didn't have any broken fingers, the window was brand new so the balancers were working properly and the insurance company still forked over $3,500. If you also guessed that she was in the process of being evicted, you would have been correct on that also.

5. The fifth and final one, the straw that broke my back. A woman that admitted to the insurance company that she was heating her home with the stove sued us because she had the oven door open and her three-year-old daughter burned her hand on the stove door. 100% her fault and the insurance company pays her $4,000 bucks and raised my rate.

By now, I was ready to blow a fuse! I did all that I could do to prevent the tenant from calling an attorney by making up addendums and having my tenants sign them, but when the tenants did call an attorney, my insurance company didn't put up any kind of fight and folded up like a lawn chair. They were quick to raise my rates but slow to defend me. Enough was enough.

I started playing hardball with the attorneys when they called and I told them that they weren't getting my insurance information and they could go to hell. I told them that if they wanted to sue me they could get in line. So they did, sue me that is. Like I said, they're rats, but rats are not stupid. When my balls were placed in a vice and I was looking at the lawsuit that they filed against me, I caved in like a fat lady with bad knees. They called my bluff and won. I shot them over my insurance information with my liability amounts in clear display and they did their thing from there.

One thing that I did notice is that whenever an attorney called me for my insurance information, the first thing that they would always ask me is if I had a fire policy or if I had liability insurance. A fire policy is naturally just a policy that covers you in the event of a fire and legally, it is all the insurance company requires you to carry. Of course, it is a lot cheaper because the insurance company is not on the hook should one of these jack asses say that they had an accident on your property. So let's say you own a property that is worth 100k and you take a mortgage on it for 60k. The minimum amount the insurance company requires you to carry is going to be 60k fire policy, which would make them whole should your property burn to the ground. Although I would recommend insuring the property for the 100k so you would get the full value of the home should it go up in smoke, the mortgage company is only going to require you to carry 60k and they don't care what you do as far as liability because that's on you.

I always carried liability insurance so the instant the words "liability policy" came out of my mouth, the attorney got a hard on and wanted me to fax a copy of the deck page over immediately. The deck page is the front page of your insurance policy. It shows who your carrier is, where they are located, how they can be reached, and most importantly, your amount of liability coverage. That's when I finally figured it out.

When my insurance policy expired that year, I did **not** renew it with Allstate who was my carrier at the time. What I did not only saved money, it chased lawyers away like my tenants run away from a mop. I called an Insurance company called "Fair Plan," which is a government run insurance company (I'll talk more about them later). I purchased a fire policy **only** for each and every one of my properties. Each property was insured for the same 100k in fire that I had carried through Allstate, but I was only paying $465 per property with Fair Plan as opposed to the $811 per property that I was paying with Allstate, although the Allstate plan covered one million in liability insurance. That is a savings of $346 per property!

When the woman at Fair Plan printed out my deck pages, they were exactly what I wanted. In the box where fire coverage amount was listed was 100k. In the box where liability amount was listed was a big fat **$0**. Now it was time to execute stage two of my "Anti Lawyer" plan.

I called around to a couple of insurance companies and told them that I was looking for a 1 million "liability blanket" or "umbrella" policy." Essentially an insurance company takes my 100 properties and puts them all into one big basket. I now have 1 million worth of insurance on each and every property in the basket. If I want to add a policy, the policy rate does not go up because I am not increasing the liability amount. Whether I have 50 or 550 properties in the basket, I am insured up to a total of 1 million per occurrence.

I found a home for the liability insurance with TechInsurance who charged me an annual premium of $1,964 with a $500 deductible for a one million dollar, commercial general liability policy. Once again, I saved $346 per property but I had to pay $1,964 for the liability insurance. By knocking off $346 bucks per property on a hundred properties, I saved $34,600 so I was more than happy to pay the $1,964 for the liability policy. The policy covers up to a one million dollar limit (per occurrence) and ten thousand in medical per claim. It also covers up to $100,000 in property damage for things such as fire damage, storm damage, and theft.

Now what I have is two separate insurance policies from two different companies. One company covered me for fire, and one company covered my liability. Just like the attorney called my bluff, now it was time for me to call theirs! It only took about three months after switching up the policies for my phone to ring.

First the tenant called me to inform me that her brother intended to sue me. Supposedly her brother was bringing a dryer down the basement steps and when he leaned against the railing and, surprise, surprise, it gave way and he fell to the floor and hurt his back. (That's funny, I eliminated the washer/dryer hook-up so where the hell were they going with the washer?) I told her to go pound sand up her ass, then her attorney called.

I held on the line listening to this bullshit, waiting for that all too familiar question. Just as sure as the sun will come out tomorrow, it came. "Do you have liability insurance?"

"**Nope,**" I responded.

"Well do you have insurance?"

"I only have a fire policy, buddy ." Of which, he of course, asked if I could fax over the policy deck page to him. I would have loved to been a fly on the wall when he read the $0 in the liability box. Anyway, my phone rang back about a half an hour later with some pretty desperate, pathetic threats.

The first bunch of lies, I cut off real fast. "You know, this guy got shook up pretty good from this fall."

"Yeah, I don't give a shit, anything else you want to tell me," I responded.

"Do you know that I can sue you personally"?

"Uh, my properties are in an LLC, so you can't."

"Well I can get a judgment and put a lien on your property."

"Be me guest, go right ahead, the line starts around the corner. I don't give a shit if you put ten liens on the property, it'll help it from falling down. Spend every cent of your money trying to score a settlement for some dirtbag because I'm never selling the property and you'll hold your hand on your ass until it turns blue if you're waiting to get a buck out of me." Then I slammed the phone down but I knew he wouldn't give up that easy. Just like a bill collector, he calls right back.

"Look, how about we settle this thing right now and I won't have to come after you. All the guy is looking for is five grand to cover his medical and future lost wages."

I laughed at him, assured him I wouldn't give him two cents, ever, and reminded him that a lien on my rental property was the least of my worries. He told me that he was going to move forward and I'd see him in court. I told him that I welcome lawsuits and it's been seven years and I have not seen hide nor hair of him, in fact I wouldn't know him if I tripped over him. I've had six more similar instances, all of which ended in the same result which was, no one filed a lawsuit on me! I am 7 for 7 since implementing the anti-lawyer plan and I'll explain to you the "why" of it.

Lawyers are a greedy bunch. Most of them went to school for seven or eight years so they could learn how to get blood from a stone. The only time that they are going to reach into their wallet to pull out a buck is if they are certain they are going to be able to reach back into your wallet to pull out ten bucks. There are costs and procedures that they will incur when they are setting up to file a lawsuit against you. First is their filing fees, yes, it costs them money to sue you. Not only that, they probably have to pay a secretary or paralegal to type the whole thing out and bring it over to the courthouse for filing.

Next, they usually have a doctor that they like sending their phony clients to. Why not send them to a phony doctor, such as a chiropractor, who is willing to play ball. What I mean by, "Play ball" is to give the attorney's clients treatment that he or she doesn't even need so they can ring up the medical bills. The only problem is that if you don't have liability coverage and the attorney doesn't get paid, the doctor isn't going to get paid either. The attorney does not want to tarnish or jeopardize his relationship with the doctor so why on earth would the attorney send him a patient that the doctor may not get paid for treating? The answer is he won't and with no medical reports or medical treatment, there won't be any lawsuits filed either.

The final reason why they won't file suit against you if you don't have liability insurance is they don't want to wait. They are not going to sue you today for money that they may or may not get twenty five years from now. Most of these ambulance chasers that run the TV commercials on the Maury and Steve Wilkos show get hundreds of calls a week from scammers that don't want to work and think that they have a case against somebody. The attorneys don't want to waste their time, effort and money, suing someone who is not insured when they have a pool of people to sue who are insured.

Now if it ever comes to be and an attorney does move forward on a lawsuit against me, which I never see happening, I'll be more than happy to send him over my one million dollar liability policy but until I open up a registered letter saying I'm a party to a lawsuit, I'm keeping my policy right where it belongs, closed!

My final thoughts on lawyers and I hope that after using this tip we never have to discuss them again. I don't know how many of you watched the series "Breaking Bad?" Awesome show! There was an attorney on the show named Saul Goodman who parlayed his role into a spin-off called, "Better Call Saul." There was a scene in one of the episodes where Saul's brother, also an attorney, is eating dinner with his girlfriend and Saul. Saul decides to rattle off a few lawyer jokes in a row which were hilarious, although his brother is a much more serious lawyer who is not enjoying the jokes, which makes it even funnier. I'd like to share a couple of my favorite lawyer jokes. I'm here all day!

1. Where can you find a good lawyer? The city morgue.

2. What's the difference between a porcupine and a Mercedes full of attorneys? The por- cupine has pricks on the outside.

3. What do you have when a lawyer is buried up to his neck in sand? Not enough sand.

4. What's the difference between a dead rat and a dead attorney in the middle of the street? The rat has skid marks in front of it.

5. How was copper wire invented? Two lawyers pulling on a penny.

6. How do you prevent an attorney from drowning? Shoot him before he goes into the water.

7. Why does the American Bar Association prohibit sex between attorneys and their clients? To prevent the client for being billed twice for what is essentially the same service.

8. What is the difference between a duck and lawyer? Occasionally a duck will stick his bill up his ass.

Well that's gonna rap it up on the attorney subject. Hope you were able to learn a little, save a lot, and most importantly, get a good laugh. Before I close this chapter, I want to go to bat for the one and only lawyer that I trust. I came in contact with him years ago when he settled my workman's compensation claim and I still to this day consider him a friend. Not only did he do a great job for me but he also helped my Dad out when my father broke his ankle. His name is Ken Schuster and he's located in Media PA. I'd trust and recommend him to anyone, he's that good!

CHAPTER 30

FAIR PLAN INSURANCE

Okay, in the previous chapter I told you that I would discuss "Fair Plan Insurance." What it basically is; is a state mandated program that provides insurance for people who are having trouble insuring their property due to the fact that their insurers consider them "high risk." It's a law that you have to be able to insure your property and Fair Plan is the outlet.

Fair Plan insurance is a state program sometimes subsidized by private insurance companies. These plans provide insurance to people that would otherwise be denied insurance on their property due to a high risk area or other related problems.

Usually high risk, when renting to Section 8 tenants, involves your property being located in a high crime area where there is a lot of vandalism, fire claims, and theft (such as copper). I have never had a problem getting insurance but a lot of people who I talk to on my website say that the second the insurer asks them, "Is the property a flat roof?" and they answer yes, the insurer wants nothing to do with them. I always refer them to Fair Plan and they end up receiving a policy.

Another time Fair Plan comes in handy is if your property has not been renovated yet and is in disrepair. Whenever I purchased a shell or a property that needed a ton of rehab, I would call Allstate and have the property added to my policy. They would bind (which means instantly cover the property) the property and schedule an inspection within 7 days. Depending on how bad a condition the property was in, the inspector would usually break my balls. Even though he could physically see me rehabbing the property he would drive violations and hazards down my throat. Wise men speak because they have something to say, fools speak because they want to say something. He would tell me, "You need a railing on these steps;" or "The service wire needs to be replaced, three concrete blocks on the sidewalk need to be repaired or replaced." Yadda, yadda, yadda. No shit Einstein, what the hell do you think I'm doing over here? I just bought the place less than a week ago! Can you give me a chance to scratch my ass? What a hassle.

Anyway, you don't get that with Fair Plan inspectors. They seemed to be much more laidback and about 80% of the time, they do drive-by inspections, my favorites! They go by in a car and if you're property isn't a burn-out or a board-up, you passed. When they do come into the property, they don't try to find things in the property "not to insure" you on. If you look hard enough at any property, you're going to find something to fail somebody on. Don't get me wrong, I'm sure that if the front steps were missing and the sidewalk looked like the moon, you might have a little trouble getting liability insurance but that's not what I use them for in the first place, just fire. For the most part "fair" is exactly what they are.

Another scenario that Fair Plan can come to the rescue on is if you have had a high number of claims on your properties. When you're in this racket, you can try to prevent claims all day long but sooner or later something is gonna get you, no doubt about it. Whether your tenant leaves a pot on the stove and sets the kitchen on fire or a 300-pound woman leans back while sitting on the toilet, cracks the tank and floods the house, something is bound to happen. When these claims start to add up, the insurance carrier will up your rate or cancel your policy so the good news here is that Fair Plan also offers theft, flood, vandalism, and liability insurance also.

Once you are cancelled from one insurance carrier, good luck finding insurance. It's almost like they blackball you, you're no longer permitted in the club. If it weren't for Fair Plan, you'd have a better chance of finding a one ended stick than you would insurance. You can try to bullshit your next potential insurance carrier and say that you never had a claim (I know because I tried it), but the way computers are today, they'll spit out the previous claims against the property you are trying to insure so quick it'll make your head spin. You won't get that with Fair Plan. Fortunately, they don't care about previous claims.

Here is the beauty of Fair Plan, the thing that I like the most. It's cheap! If you went out and totaled three cars this month, your auto rates would skyrocket or your carrier would drop you, either or. You'd pick up the phone and call another insurance company. They'd look at your driving record and tell you to get a bicycle. Even though we are talking about houses as opposed to cars here, Fair Plan doesn't work that way, thank God! I can walk into their office trying to insure a property that has caught on fire, had a flood, and has been vandalized and I will still receive a lower quote than what I was getting from Allstate. The exact rate that I am paying for a 100k fire, theft, and vandalism policy (no liability), today, March 15th 2017, is $465. What a deal. Tell'em Mike sent you so I can get my referral fee. LOL, I'm just playing with you. I talked about Fair Plan so much that it sounds like I've got stock in the joint but when I find a person or a company who is a straight shooter; I like to share it with my readers and give that person or company their props!

CHAPTER 31

TALK TO ME!

Okay, you've purchased the books, read them, and now you have a question, or in some cases, a lot of questions that you would like to ask me. Well now you can fire away! I've created a new link on my website where you can schedule a one on one phone conversation with the king of Section 8 Landlording. Whether you want to bounce some questions off of me about what you've read, ask me advice on what it is you are doing, plan a strategy on how to get rid of a tenant, put a blueprint together on how to build an empire, or simply share a couple of stories and laughs about your experiences in the crazy world of Section 8 Landlording, I'm sure that I can help you.

With me as your mentor, I'll save you money by sharing my knowledge and in fact, I'm rather quite cheap! Most real estate mentors want you to sign up for a $5,000 to $8,000 course and travel to wherever it is that they are holding their "seminar." Me, I only charge $59 bucks. These other guys want to stick you in an auditorium with 100 other suckers, hand you a couple of manuals that they charge you a hundred bucks for, tell you how rich you are going to be, and then call it a day. You'll never get any one on one time with them and if you have a question to ask them, you'll probably have to wait until the 50 people in front of you get done asking their question. How do I know? Because yours truly got suckered into a three-day course in Florida back in 2009 on how to "cash in" on all the Florida foreclosures. I would have gotten more out of wrestling an alligator down there. I packed it up after five hours of their bogus course and took the loss. They tried to upsell me everything under the sun from more "technical courses," to round trip airline tickets back and forth to Florida. Hell, I think they even charged me for the pen I was using. The best thing that I got out of the entire adventure was a tan. I won't ask you to purchase one thing from me during our phone conversation, I simply want to do my best in getting any questions that you have for me answered.

I'm not trying to sell you on anything other than myself. You've read my books they are very easy to understand, and your phone call will be the same way. The conversation will also be the same as my books, relaxed and loose. I won't come across like those arrogant guys on the Saturday morning infomercials. I'm very personable and if you thought enough of me to pay for a phone call, then I'm going to do my very best to make it worth your while. I'm also sure we'll get a laugh or two during our conversation, I always do. Here is how it works:

1. I charge $59.95 for a half hour and $99 for an hour. Minimum purchase is a half hour.

2. Once you have made the purchase, I will email you within 24 hours to schedule our conversation. Whether you are east

coast, west coast, or in Hawaii, we'll work it out and agree to an appointment time. Our appointment will be scheduled no later than five days after you have made your purchase.

3. Once we agree to a time, I will call you on time, every time!

4. Just like your email address, I will not share your phone number with anyone, under any circumstances.

I truly love talking about real estate; I just hate emailing back and forth all night with people who have questions about the book. It's so impersonal and time consuming and by the end of the night I feel like my fingers are going to fall off. I'd rather talk one on one with you. I feel as though you will get more out of a phone call as opposed to an email, and of course getting paid a little for my time doesn't hurt either. I don't need $59 bucks that bad; in fact, I'd pay $59 bucks to watch two flies screw but the reason I do these calls is because I **enjoy doing them!** Try buying a book off of someone else and getting two minutes of their time, it's not gonna happen. I'll never bullshit you either, if there is a question that I don't know the answer to, I'll let you know. I've got the answers to 99% of them but every once in a while somebody throws me a curveball. So if you have any questions, bring 'em on. Let's do this!

Let's talk!

A NOTE FROM MIKE ON FEBRUARY 2020

Hey gang,

It's Mike McLean and I want to personally thank you for your purchase of Volume 3, I hope it saves you money and I really hope that you enjoyed it. Just like I do on the last page of all my books, I'll give you a little insight on how Volume 3 originated.

After releasing Volumes 1 and 2 of the Section 8 Bible, I wasn't even planning on writing a Volume 3. The first two books were still selling well and to be honest, the mistakes that I was making were few and far between now, which made it harder to come up with material. I'll never, ever just write to fill up pages! If the content has no substance, it'll bore me writing about it and you'll stop buying my books and that's the last thing that I want to happen. Secondly, I just got so busy purchasing, rehabbing, flipping, and renting that I didn't have time to scratch my ass. Before I knew it, ten years blew by faster than you could say I. For some strange reason at about that time, a light bulb went off in my head the read, "Hey Mike, I think you have enough material for a book now," so I started writing again!

Let me say this, after my ten-year hiatus, I absolutely loved, loved, loved writing Volume 3 and it's probably my personal favorite of all 3 of my books. Why? Because I didn't realize, until I picked up the pen again, how much I love to write. I sit back and read some of this shit and I have got to laugh at myself. I try to remember exactly how an experience happened, what lesson was learned, then I put it into words. By the time I turn the light off to go to bed, I have five or six pages of material that didn't exist two hours ago. It's such a satisfying feeling.

Some guys write books to get rich, they don't care what the hell they tell you, just as long as they can suck you in with false promises and get more money out of you. That's not me! You'll never hear me invite you to my $1,500 seminar with limited seating, so "act quickly." I'm not holding a $2,000 conference where I'm looking for only a selected few people who want to learn how to buy real estate using other people's money and no money down. No, these guys are full of shit and their full-time gig is bullshitting and hustling people out of their money. They're salesmen, not landlords and I'd bet they've never owned rental properties in their life.

With me, as you've learned, all you have to do is put out a couple bucks and you've bought yourself the best education that you're ever going to get in the field of Section 8 Housing and that I guarantee! I took pride in writing these three books, I truly and greatly appreciate your purchases and loyalty, and I hope that you put these books to good use and get involved, you'll never go wrong with real estate. Remember this, in the end, we only regret the chances that we didn't take!

"THE GREATEST TOOL A LANDLORD CAN OWN IS AN AIRTIGHT LEASE"

After losing one too many eviction hearings, I realized that every lease I had purchased wasn't worth the paper it was printed on! So, I designed the Bulletproof Lease to protect me and my property.

My lease is packed with 41 terms and 14 addendums that protect you in easy-to-read English (so you won't have to worry about some fancy lawyer trying to use your words against you.) The addendums protect you more because the tenant must sign each and every one.

When I started out, I was using a lease that simply stated that the tenant would be responsible to replace any and all broken windows. Simple enough, right?

Wrong!

This one tenant had four broken windows that he refused to repair. His neighbors told me that his girlfriend had locked him out, and he went nuts. When I took him to court, the tenant claimed that kids playing baseball broke the windows—all four. Well, the judge bought the tenant's story and I was stuck with the tenant and the repair bill.

Now, my tenants must sign the "Broken Window Addendum." It's as simple as getting a signature, and I don't get any more broken window calls!

I'm currently using this exact lease on all 300 of my investment properties and I will never go back to a flimsy generic lease again.

I designed it, I use it, and I stand by it! It's your money and your investment, so play by your rules, not the tenant's! I guarantee that you will never think of using a generic lease again.

Get it at: www.shoptly.com/bulletprooflease

CONTACTS

Before I share all of my social media contacts with you, I'll tell you that I just got them up and running. I'll be posting a couple of videos and tips a month in the beginning but once I get started, the tips and stories will be more frequent so friend me on Facebook, subscribe to my YouTube channel, and follow me on Twitter. It's going to be a lot of fun!

Section8bible.com

Friend me on Facebook @ Section 8 Bible

Subscribe to my YouTube Channel @ Section 8 Bible

Follow me on Twitter @ MikeMcLean@Section8Mike

Email me @ section8bible@yahoo.com

I'm also on Instagram @ Section 8 Bible

DEDICATION

This book is dedicated to
Nick's brother, Joe, who passed away in 2015.
Joe, you will be missed!

Nick and Joe Cipriano

Made in the USA
Monee, IL
30 January 2024

52653117R00118